Hands-On Artificial Intelligence for Search

Building intelligent applications and perform enterprise searches

Devangini Patel

BIRMINGHAM - MUMBAI

Hands-On Artificial Intelligence for Search

Copyright © 2018 Packt Publishing

Commissioning Editor: Sunith Shetty
Acquisition Editor: Akshay Jethani
Content Development Editor: Abhishek Jadhav
Technical Editor: Swathy Mohan
Copy Editor: Safis Editing
Project Coordinator: Jagdish Prabhu
Proofreader: Safis Editing
Indexer: Tejal Daruwale Soni
Graphics: Tom Scaria
Production Coordinator: Shantanu Zagade

First published: August 2018

Production reference: 1290818

Published by Packt Publishing Ltd.
Livery Place
35 Livery Street
Birmingham
B3 2PB, UK.

ISBN 978-1-78961-115-1

www.packtpub.com

`mapt.io`

Mapt is an online digital library that gives you full access to over 5,000 books and videos, as well as industry leading tools to help you plan your personal development and advance your career. For more information, please visit our website.

Why subscribe?

- Spend less time learning and more time coding with practical eBooks and Videos from over 4,000 industry professionals

- Improve your learning with Skill Plans built especially for you

- Get a free eBook or video every month

- Mapt is fully searchable

- Copy and paste, print, and bookmark content

PacktPub.com

Did you know that Packt offers eBook versions of every book published, with PDF and ePub files available? You can upgrade to the eBook version at `www.PacktPub.com` and as a print book customer, you are entitled to a discount on the eBook copy. Get in touch with us at `service@packtpub.com` for more details.

At `www.PacktPub.com`, you can also read a collection of free technical articles, sign up for a range of free newsletters, and receive exclusive discounts and offers on Packt books and eBooks.

Contributors

About the author

Devangini Patel is a PhD student at the National University of Singapore, Singapore. Her research interests include deep learning, computer vision, machine learning, and artificial intelligence. She has completed a master's in artificial intelligence at the University of Southampton, UK. She has over 5 years, experience in the field of AI and has worked on various industrial and research projects in AI, including facial expression analysis, robotics, virtual try-on, object recognition and detection, and advertisement ranking.

About the reviewer

Nisarg Vyas is the CEO, founder, and principal engineer at InFoCusp, a consultancy firm in Ahmedabad specializing in AI projects. For the past 12 years, he has been associated with introducing AI and automated systems into mainstream products for domains such as physiological monitoring and healthcare, wearable computing, finance, recruitment and HR, e-commerce, law, defense, graphics, gaming, pharmaceuticals, and fishing. His contribution to AI for physiological monitoring was featured in the prestigious AI Magazine and acknowledged by the Association for the Advancement of AI (AAAI) as an innovative application of AI. He is the holder of several US patents, and the author of several peer-reviewed journal and conference publications.

Packt is searching for authors like you

If you're interested in becoming an author for Packt, please visit `authors.packtpub.com` and apply today. We have worked with thousands of developers and tech professionals, just like you, to help them share their insight with the global tech community. You can make a general application, apply for a specific hot topic that we are recruiting an author for, or submit your own idea.

Table of Contents

Preface   1

Chapter 1: Understanding the Depth-First Search Algorithm   5
  Installing and setting up libraries   5
    Setting up Python   6
    Setting up Graphviz   8
    Installing pip   12
  Introduction to file searching applications   14
  Basic search concepts   16
  Formulating the search problem   17
  Building trees with nodes   22
  Stack data structure   27
  The DFS algorithm   29
    Recursive DFS   35
  Do it yourself   44
  Summary   44

Chapter 2: Understanding the Breadth-First Search Algorithm   45
  Understanding the LinkedIn connection feature   46
  Graph data structure   51
  Queue data structure   55
  The BFS algorithm   57
  BFS versus DFS   63
    Order of traversal   63
    Data structures   64
    Memory   64
    Optimal solution   65
  Do it yourself   66
  Summary   68

Chapter 3: Understanding the Heuristic Search Algorithm   69
  Revisiting the navigation application   70
  The priority queue data structure   72
  Visualizing a search tree   75
  Greedy BFS   84
  A* Search   93
  What is a good heuristic function?   103
    Properties of a good heuristic function   103
      Admissible   103
      Consistent   105

Summary   107

Other Books You May Enjoy   109

Index   113

Preface

With the emergence of big data and modern technologies, artificial intelligence (AI) has acquired a lot of relevance in many domains. The increase in demand for automation has generated many applications for AI in fields such as robotics, predictive analytics, and finance.

This book will give you an understanding of what AI is. It explains basic search methods in detail: Depth-First Search (DFS), Breadth-First Search (BFS), and A* Search, which can be used to make intelligent decisions when the initial state, end state, and possible actions are known. Random solutions or greedy solutions can be found for such problems, but they are not optimal in terms of either space or time, and efficient approaches to space and time will be explored. We will also look at how to formulate a problem, which involves identifying its initial state, goal state, and the actions that are possible in each state. We also need to understand the data structures involved while implementing these search algorithms, because they form the basis of search exploration. Finally, we will look into what a heuristic is, because this decides the suitability of one sub-solution over another and helps you decide which step to take.

Who this book is for

This book is for developers who are keen to get started with AI and develop practical AI-based applications. Developers who want to upgrade their normal applications to smart and intelligent versions will find this book useful. A basic knowledge and understanding of Python are assumed.

What this book covers

Chapter 1, *Understanding the Depth-First Search Algorithm*, practically explains the DFS algorithm with the help of a search tree. The chapter also delves into recursion, which eliminates the need to have an explicit stack.

Chapter 2, *Understanding the Breadth-First Search Algorithm*, teaches you how to traverse a graph layer-wise using a LinkedIn connection feature as an example.

Chapter 3, *Understanding the Heuristic Search Algorithm*, takes you through the priority queue data structure and explains how to visualize search trees. The chapter also covers problems related to greedy best-first search, and how A* solves that problem.

To get the most out of this book

The software requirements for running the codes are as follows:

- Python 2.7.6
- Pydot and Matplotlib libraries
- LiClipse

Download the example code files

You can download the example code files for this book from your account at `www.packtpub.com`. If you purchased this book elsewhere, you can visit `www.packtpub.com/support` and register to have the files emailed directly to you.

You can download the code files by following these steps:

1. Log in or register at `www.packtpub.com`.
2. Select the **SUPPORT** tab.
3. Click on **Code Downloads & Errata**.
4. Enter the name of the book in the **Search** box and follow the onscreen instructions.

Once the file is downloaded, please make sure that you unzip or extract the folder using the latest version of:

- WinRAR/7-Zip for Windows
- Zipeg/iZip/UnRarX for Mac
- 7-Zip/PeaZip for Linux

The code bundle for the book is also hosted on GitHub at **https://github.com/PacktPublishing/Hands-On-Artificial-Intelligence-for-Search**. In case there's an update to the code, it will be updated on the existing GitHub repository.

We also have other code bundles from our rich catalog of books and videos available at `https://github.com/PacktPublishing/`. Check them out!

Download the color images

We also provide a PDF file that has color images of the screenshots/diagrams used in this book. You can download it here: https://www.packtpub.com/sites/default/files/downloads/HandsOnArtificialIntelligenceforSearch_ColorImages.pdf.

Conventions used

There are a number of text conventions used throughout this book.

CodeInText: Indicates code words in text, database table names, folder names, filenames, file extensions, pathnames, dummy URLs, user input, and Twitter handles. Here is an example: "The State class has to be changed for every application, even though the search algorithm is the same."

A block of code is set as follows:

```
def checkGoalState(self):
        """
        This method checks whether the person is Jill.
        """
        #check if the person's name is Jill
        return self.name == "Jill"
```

When we wish to draw your attention to a particular part of a code block, the relevant lines or items are set in bold:

```
#create a dictionary with all the mappings
connections = {}
connections["Dev"] = {"Ali", "Seth", "Tom"}
connections["Ali"] = {"Dev", "Seth", "Ram"}
connections["Seth"] = {"Ali", "Tom", "Harry"}
connections["Tom"] = {"Dev", "Seth", "Kai", 'Jill'}
connections["Ram"] = {"Ali", "Jill"}
```

Any command-line input or output is written as follows:

```
$ pip install pydot
```

Bold: Indicates a new term, an important word, or words that you see onscreen. For example, words in menus or dialog boxes appear in the text like this. Here is an example: "Select **System info** from the **Administration** panel."

Warnings or important notes appear like this.

 Tips and tricks appear like this.

Get in touch

Feedback from our readers is always welcome.

General feedback: Email feedback@packtpub.com and mention the book title in the subject of your message. If you have questions about any aspect of this book, please email us at questions@packtpub.com.

Errata: Although we have taken every care to ensure the accuracy of our content, mistakes do happen. If you have found a mistake in this book, we would be grateful if you would report this to us. Please visit www.packtpub.com/submit-errata, selecting your book, clicking on the Errata Submission Form link, and entering the details.

Piracy: If you come across any illegal copies of our works in any form on the Internet, we would be grateful if you would provide us with the location address or website name. Please contact us at copyright@packtpub.com with a link to the material.

If you are interested in becoming an author: If there is a topic that you have expertise in and you are interested in either writing or contributing to a book, please visit authors.packtpub.com.

Reviews

Please leave a review. Once you have read and used this book, why not leave a review on the site that you purchased it from? Potential readers can then see and use your unbiased opinion to make purchase decisions, we at Packt can understand what you think about our products, and our authors can see your feedback on their book. Thank you!

For more information about Packt, please visit packtpub.com.

1
Understanding the Depth-First Search Algorithm

Search algorithms have various applications in industrial and research-based AI solutions, related to computer vision, machine learning, and robotics. As we progress through the chapters in this book, we will teach you how to use AI in search applications. Searching is something that we do every day, whether we are searching for a song in our filesystem, searching for a friend or colleague on a social network, or finding the best route to a destination. In this chapter, you will learn about the **Depth-First Search** (**DFS**) algorithm and develop a file search application.

In this chapter, we will cover the following topics:

- Installing and setting up libraries
- Introducing file search applications
- Formulation of the search problem
- Building search trees with nodes
- Stacks and DFS
- Recursive DFS

Installing and setting up libraries

Before we get into the basic concepts of searching, we will take a look at the following libraries that have to be installed and how to install them in Windows:

- **Python**: You can download and install Python libraries from `https://www.python.org/downloads/`, depending on your operating system
- **Graphviz**: This open source graph visualization software can be downloaded from `http://graphviz.org/download/`

- **Pip**: The tools for installing Python packages are as follows:
  - **Pydot**: A Python interface to Graphviz's DOT language
  - **Matplotlib**: This is a Python 2D plotting library

Execute the steps in the following section to install the preceding libraries.

Setting up Python

The steps for setting up Python are as follows:

1. For the applications in this book, we'll be using Python 2.7.6, which we can download from `https://www.python.org/downloads/`.
2. Once an appropriate installer has been downloaded, double-click on it and go ahead with the default options.
3. Based on your operating system, select the Python installer to download, as shown in the following screenshot:

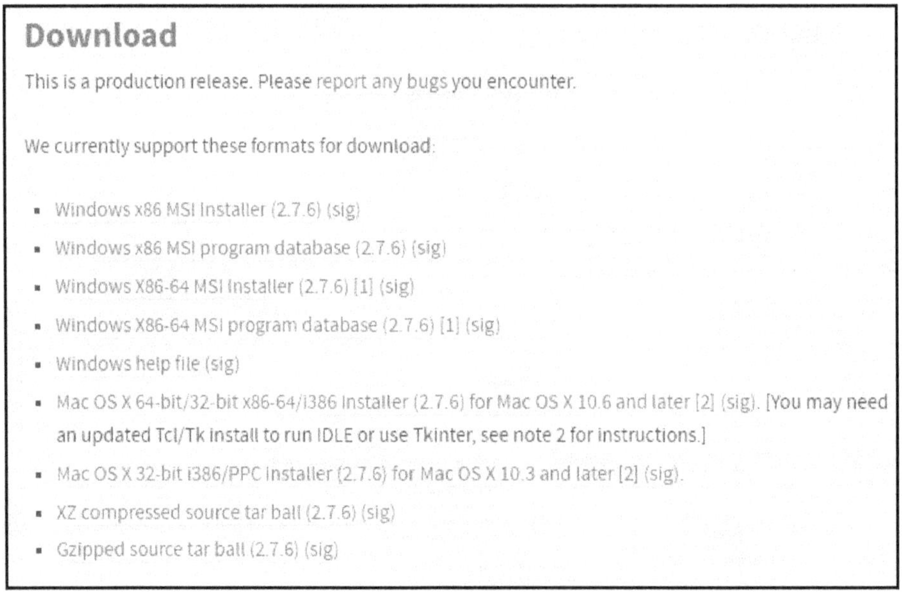

Download

This is a production release. Please report any bugs you encounter.

We currently support these formats for download:

- Windows x86 MSI Installer (2.7.6) (sig)
- Windows x86 MSI program database (2.7.6) (sig)
- Windows X86-64 MSI Installer (2.7.6) [1] (sig)
- Windows X86-64 MSI program database (2.7.6) [1] (sig)
- Windows help file (sig)
- Mac OS X 64-bit/32-bit x86-64/i386 Installer (2.7.6) for Mac OS X 10.6 and later [2] (sig). [You may need an updated Tcl/Tk install to run IDLE or use Tkinter, see note 2 for instructions.]
- Mac OS X 32-bit i386/PPC Installer (2.7.6) for Mac OS X 10.3 and later [2] (sig).
- XZ compressed source tar ball (2.7.6) (sig)
- Gzipped source tar ball (2.7.6) (sig)

Figure 1

4. The following screenshot shows the location where Python will be installed; make a note of this location:

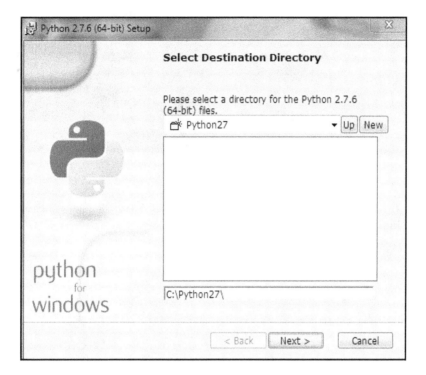

Figure 2

Now, Python will be installed.

5. The next step is to add Python's path to the **Path** environment variable. In the **System Properties | Advanced** tab, click on the **Environment Variables...** button.

6. In the **Environment Variables...** window, go to **System variables | Path** and add the Python location that you made a note of in step 4 (which is C:\Python27 in our case).

7. Now, to check whether Python works, open the Command Prompt and type in the `python -- version` command. You will get the following output:

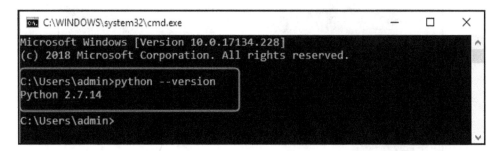

Figure 3

The output shown in the preceding screenshot confirms that Python has been installed successfully.

Depending on your OS, Python might already be installed.

Setting up Graphviz

The following steps describe how to set up Graphviz:

1. We can download the graph visualization software from `https://graphviz.gitlab.io/download/`.

2. Since we are using Windows, we select the option that says **Stable 2.38 Windows install packages**, as shown in the following screenshot:

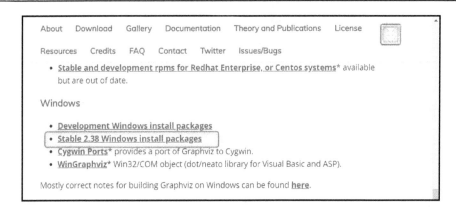

Figure 4

Select the .msi downloadable file, shown as follows:

Figure 5

3. Once the Graphviz executable has downloaded, go ahead and install the file with the default options; again, make a note of the path, as shown in the following screenshot:

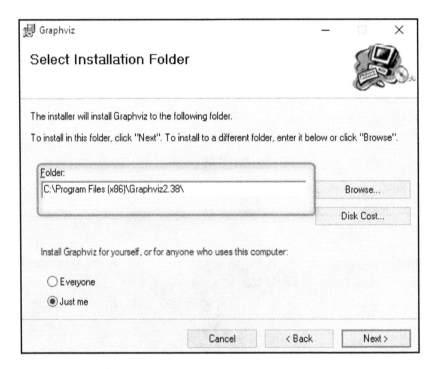

Figure 6

4. Now, we will add Graphviz's `bin` folder to the path variable, as we did when installing Python in the previous section. Then, copy the location where Graphviz is installed and append `\bin`, as shown in the following screenshot:

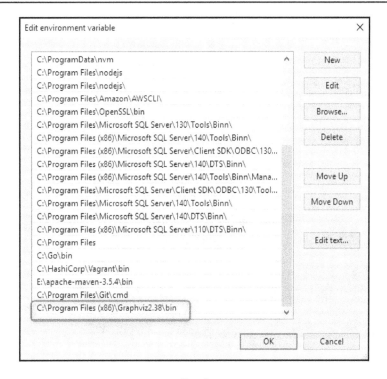

Figure 7

5. To validate whether this library has been installed properly, open a new Command Prompt window and type the `dot -V` command, and you will get the following result:

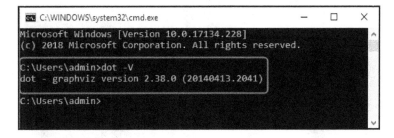

Figure 8

The output shown in the preceding screenshot confirms that Graphviz has been installed successfully.

Installing pip

The steps for installing `pip` are as follows:

1. To install `pip`, you need to download the `get-pip.py` file from `https://bootstrap.pypa.io/get-pip.py`, and make a note of the path where the file is located. In my case, the file is located at `Documents\ai\softwares`.

2. Open the Command Prompt and go to the `Documents\ai\softwares` folder by using the `cd` command, as shown in the following screenshot:

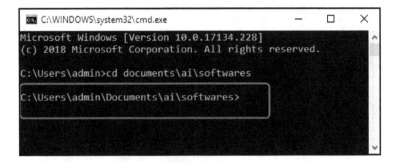

Figure 9

3. Use the `dir` command to take a look at the contents of this folder, where you will see `get-pip.py`, shown in the following screenshot:

```
C:\WINDOWS\system32\cmd.exe                              -    □    ×
Microsoft Windows [Version 10.0.17134.228]
(c) 2018 Microsoft Corporation. All rights reserved.

C:\Users\admin>cd documents\ai\softwares

C:\Users\admin\Documents\ai\softwares>dir
 Volume in drive C has no label.
 Volume Serial Number is 9A21-5F26

 Directory of C:\Users\admin\Documents\ai\softwares

16-08-2018  13:12    <DIR>          .
16-08-2018  13:12    <DIR>
16-08-2018  13:12         1,642,522 get-pip.py
               1 File(s)     1,642,522 bytes
               2 Dir(s)  37,351,018,496 bytes free

C:\Users\admin\Documents\ai\softwares>
```

Figure 10

4. Next, we'll run the `python get-pip.py` command.

5. Now, let's add Python's `scripts` folder to the **Path** environment variable.

6. Open another Command Prompt window and test the installation of `pip` by typing the `pip --version` command. Upon successful installation, you will get the following output:

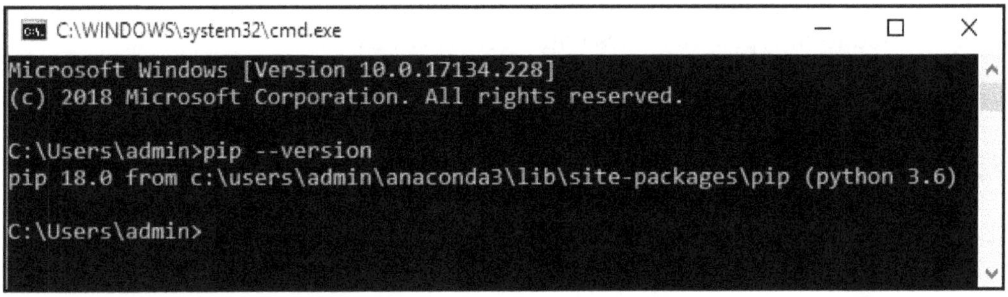

Figure 11

7. Once `pip` has installed, you can install `pydot` by running the following command:

```
pip install pydot
```

8. Finally, install `matplotlib` by executing the following command:

```
pip install matplotlib
```

9. We can check whether the libraries have been installed properly by using the `import` command in Python's interpreter, as shown in the following screenshot:

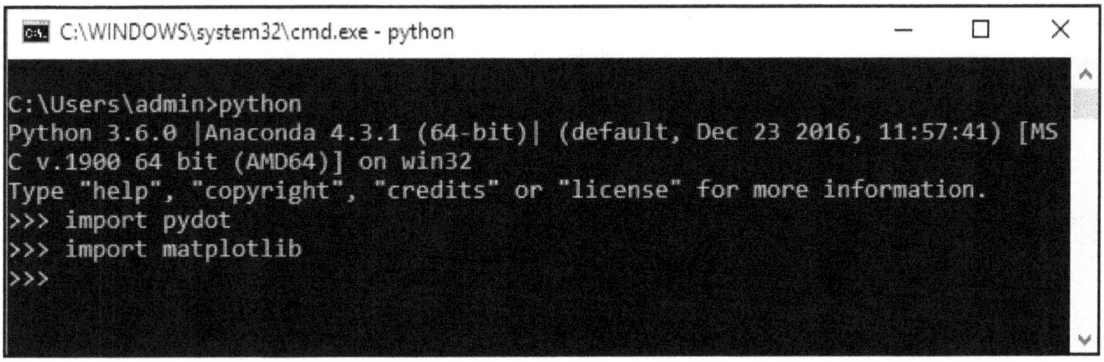

Figure 12

Now, we're done installing the libraries that we will need in Windows for this book . In the next topic, we will look at how we can go about developing a file search application.

Introduction to file searching applications

In file managers, file searching is used to find files with specific names. In IDEs, file searching is used to find program files with specific code text.

In this topic, we'll develop the first example in order to find a file named `f211.txt`. The folder structure is shown in the following screenshot:

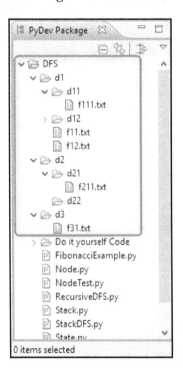

Figure 13

This folder structure can be represented as a tree, as shown in the following diagram; the file that we're trying to find is shown with a green border:

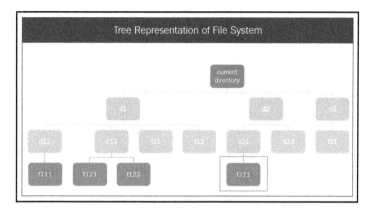

Figure 14

Let's go ahead and look at how file searching will work to find this file:

1. File searching starts in the **current directory**; it opens the first folder inside of that (**d1**) and opens the first folder in **d1** (**d11**). Inside of **d11**, it compares all of the filenames.

2. Since there's no more content inside of **d11**, the algorithm gets out of **d11**, goes inside of **d1**, and goes for the next folder, which is **d12**, comparing all of its files.

3. Now, it moves outside of **d12** and goes for the next folder inside of **d1** (**f11**), and then the next folder (**f12**).

4. Now, the search algorithm has covered all of the contents inside of the **d1** folder. So, it gets out of **d1** and goes for the next folder inside of the **current directory**, which is **d2**.

5. Inside of **d2**, it opens the first folder (**d21**). Inside of **d21**, it compares all of the files, and we find the **f211** file that we're looking for.

If you refer to the preceding folder structure, you will see that there's a pattern that is being repeated. When we reached **f111**, the algorithm had explored the leftmost part of the tree, upto its maximum depth. Once the maximum depth was reached, the algorithm backtracked to the previous level and went for the next subtree to the right. Again, in this case, the leftmost part of the subtree is explored, and, when we reach the maximum depth, the algorithm goes for the next subtree. This process is repeated until the file that we are searching for is found.

Now that we understand how the search algorithm functions logically, in the next topic, we will go through the main ingredients of searching, which are used for performing searching in this application.

Basic search concepts

To understand the functionality of search algorithms, we first need to understand basic searching concepts, such as the state, the ingredients of a search, and the nodes:

- **State**: The state is defined as the space where the search process takes place. It basically answers the question—*what are we searching for?* For example, in a navigation application, a state is a place. In our search application, a state is a file or folder.
- **Ingredients of a search**: There are three main ingredients in a search algorithm. These ingredients are as follows, using the example of a treasure hunt:
    - **Initial state**: This answers the question—*where do we begin our search?* In our example, the initial state would be the location where we begin our treasure hunt.
    - **Successor function**: This answers the question—*how do we explore from the initial state?* In our example, the successor function should return all of the paths from the location where we began our treasure hunt.
    - **Goal function**: This answers the question—*how will we know when we've found the solution?* In our example, the goal function returns true if you've found the place marked as the treasure.

The search ingredients are illustrated in the following diagram:

Ingredients of Searching

Initial State
Where do we start searching from?

Successor Function
How do we explore from current state?

Goal Function
How do we know we found the solution?

Figure 15

- **Node**: A node is the basic unit of a tree. It may consist of data or links to other nodes.

Formulating the search problem

In a file searching application, we start searching from the current directory, so our initial state is the current directory. Now, let's write the code for the state and the initial state, as follows:

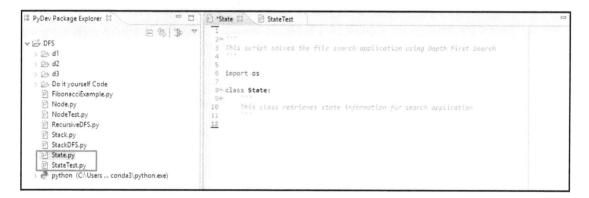

Figure 16

In the preceding screenshot, we have created two Python modules, State.py and StateTest.py. The State.py module will contain the code for the three search ingredients mentioned in the previous section. The StateTest module is a file where we can test these ingredients.

Let's go ahead and create a constructor and a function that returns an initial state, as shown in the following code:

```
....
import os

class State:
    '''
    This class retrieves state information for search application
    '''
    def __init__(self, path = None):
        if path == None:
            #create initial state
            self.path = self.getInitialState()
        else:
            self.path = path
    def getInitialState(self):
        """
        This method returns the current directory
        """
        initialState = os.path.dirname(os.path.realpath(__file__))
        return initialState
....
```

In the preceding code, the following apply:

- We have the constructor (the constructor name) and we have created a property called path, which stores the actual path of the state. In the preceding code example, we can see that the constructor takes path as an argument. The if...else block suggests that if the path is not provided, it will initialize the state as the initial state, and if the path is provided, it will create a state with that particular path.
- The getInitialState() function returns the current working directory.

Now, let's go ahead and create some sample states, as follows:

```
...
from State import State
import os
import pprint
```

```
initialState = State()
print "initialState", initialState.path

interState = State(os.path.join(initialState.path, "d2", "d21"))
goalState = State(os.path.join(initialState.path, "d2", "d21", "f211.txt"))

print "interState", interState.path
print "goalState", goalState.path
. . . .
```

In the preceding code, we have created the following three states:

- initialState, which points to the current directory
- interState, which is the intermediate function that points to the d21 folder
- goalState, which points to the f211.txt folder

Next, we will look at the successor function. If we're in a particular folder, the successor function should return the folders and files inside of that folder, and, if you're currently looking at a file, it should return an empty array. Considering the following diagram, if the current state is d2, it should return paths to the d21 and d22 folders:

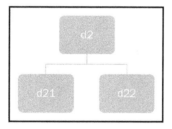

Figure 17

Now, let's create the preceding function with the following code:

```
...
    def successorFunction(self):
        """
        This is the successor function. It generates all the possible
        paths that can be reached from current path.
        """
```

```
        if os.path.isdir(self.path):
            return [os.path.join(self.path, x) for x in
            sorted(os.listdir(self.path))]
        else:
            return []
    ...
```

The preceding function checks whether the current path is a directory. If it is a directory, it gets a sorted list of all of the folders and files inside it, and prepends the current path to them. If it is a file, it returns an empty array.

Now, let's test this function with some input. Open the StateTest module and take a look at the successors to the initial state and intermediate state:

```
...
initialState = State()
print "initialState", initialState.path

interState = State(os.path.join(initialState.path, "d2", "d21"))
goalState = State(os.path.join(initialState.path, "d2", "d21", "f211.txt"))

print "interState", interState.path
print "goalState", goalState.path
...
```

As shown in the preceding code, the successors to the current directory (or the initial state) are the LiClipse project files and the folders d1, d2, and d3, and the successor of the intermediate state is the f211.txt file.

The output of running the preceding code is shown in the following screenshot:

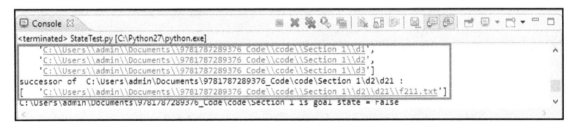

Figure 18

Finally, we will look at the goal function. So, how do we know that we have found the target file, `f211.txt`? Our goal function should return `False` for the `d21` folder, and `True` for the `f211.txt` file . Let's look at how to implement this function in code:

```
. . .
def checkGoalState(self):
        """
        This method checks whether the path is goal state
        """
        #check if it is a folder
        if os.path.isdir(self.path):
            return False
        else:
            #extract the filename
            fileSeparatorIndex = self.path.rfind(os.sep)
            filename = self.path[fileSeparatorIndex + 1 : ]
            if filename == "f211.txt":
                return True
            else:
                return False
. . .
```

As shown in the preceding code, the function `checkGoalState()` is our goal function; this checks whether the current path is a directory. Now, since we are looking for a file, this returns `False` if it's a directory. If it is a file, it extracts the filename from the path. The filename is the substring of the path from the last occurrence of a slash to the end of the string. So, we extract the filename and compare it with `f211.txt`. If they match, we return `True`; otherwise, we return `False`.

Again, let's test this function for the states that we've created. To do so, open the `StateTest` module, as shown in the following screenshot:

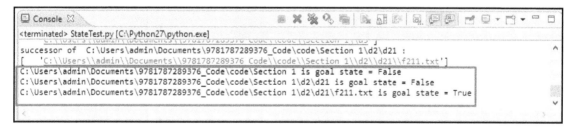

Figure 19

As you can see, the function returns `False` for the current directory, it returns `False` for the `d21` folder, and it returns `True` for the `f211.txt` file.

Now that we understand the three ingredients in search algorithms, in the next section, we will look at building search trees with nodes.

Building trees with nodes

In this topic, you'll be learning how to create a search tree with nodes. We will look at the concepts of states and nodes and the properties and methods of the node class, and we will show you how to create a tree with node objects. In our application, while the state is the path of the file or folder we are processing (for example, the current directory), the node is a node in the search tree (for example, the current directory node).

A node has many properties, and one of them is the state. The other properties are as follows:

- **Depth**: This is the level of the node in the tree
- **Reference to the parent node**: This consists of links to the parent node
- **References to the child nodes**: This consists of links to the child nodes

Let's look at a few examples, in order to understand these concepts more clearly:

- An example of these concepts in the **current directory** node is as follows:
  - **Depth**: 0
  - **Reference to parent node**: None
  - **References to children nodes**: d1, d2, d3

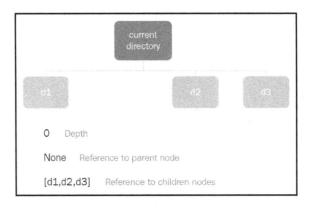

Figure 20

- An example of these concepts in node **d3** is as follows:
  - **Depth**: 1
  - **Reference to parent node**: Current directory node
  - **Reference to children nodes**: f31

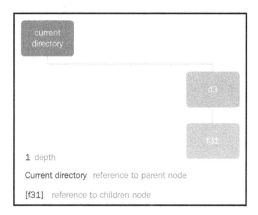

Figure 21

- An example of the concepts for these file node **f111** is as follows:
  - **Depth**: 3
  - **Reference to parent node**: d11
  - **Reference to children node**: []

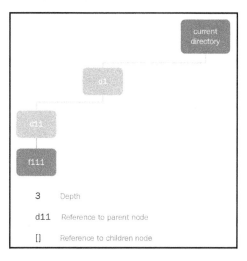

Figure 22

Let's create a class called `Node`, which includes the four properties that we just discussed:

```python
...
class Node:
    '''
    This class represents a node in the search tree
    '''
    def __init__(self, state):
        """
        Constructor
        """
        self.state = state
        self.depth = 0
        self.children = []
        self.parent = None
...
```

As shown in the preceding code, we have created a class called `Node`, and this class has a constructor that takes `state` as an argument. The `state` argument is assigned to the `state` property of this node, and the other properties are initialized as follows:

- The depth is set to `0`
- The reference to children is set to a blank array
- The reference to parent nodes is set to `None`

This constructor creates a blank node for the search tree.

Aside from the constructor, we need to create the following two methods:

- `addChild()`: This method adds a child node under a parent node
- `printTree()`: This method prints a tree structure

Consider the following code for the `addChild()` function:

```python
def addChild(self, childNode):
    """
    This method adds a node under another node
    """
    self.children.append(childNode)
    childNode.parent = self
    childNode.depth = self.depth + 1
```

The `addChild()` method takes the child node as an argument; the child node is added to the children array, and the parent of the child node is assigned as its parent node. The depth of the child node is the parent node plus one.

Let's look at this in the form of a block diagram for a clearer understanding:

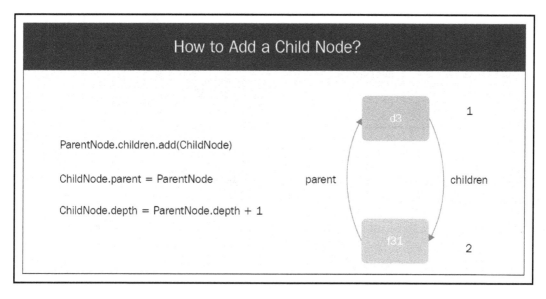

Figure 23

Let's suppose that we're adding node **f31** under node **d3**. So, **f31** will be added to the `children` property of **d3**, and the parent property of **f31** will be assigned as **d3**. In addition to that, the depth of the child node will be one more than the parent node. Here, the depth of node **d3** is **1**, so the depth of **f31** is **2**.

Let's look at the `printTree` function, as follows:

```
def printTree(self):
    """
    This method prints the tree
    """
    print self.depth , " - " , self.state.path
    for child in self.children:
        child.printTree()
```

First, this function prints the depth and the state of the current node; then, it looks through all of its children and calls the `printTree` method for each of them.

Let's try to create the search tree shown in the following diagram:

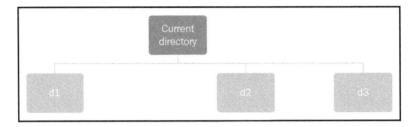

Figure 24

As shown in the preceding diagram, as a root node we have the **Current directory** node; under that node, we have nodes **d1**, **d2**, and **d3**.

We will create a `NodeTest` module, which will create the sample search tree:

```
. . .
from Node import Node
from State import State

initialState = State()
root = Node(initialState)

childStates = initialState.successorFunction()
for childState in childStates:
    childNode = Node(State(childState))
    root.addChild(childNode)
root.printTree()
. . .
```

As shown in the preceding code, we created an initial state by creating a `State` object with no arguments, and then we passed this initial state to the `Node` class constructor, which creates a root node. To get the folders `d1`, `d2`, and `d3`, we called the `successorFunction` method on the initial state and we looped each of the child states (to create a node from each of them); we added each child node under the root node.

When we execute the preceding code, we get the following output:

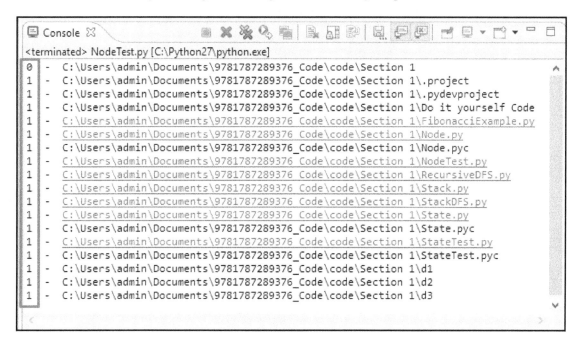

Figure 25

Here, we can see that the current directory has a depth of `0`, and all of its contents have a depth `1`, including `d1`, `d2`, and `d3`.

With that, we have successfully built a sample search tree using the `Node` class.

In the next topic, you'll be learning about the stack data structure, which will help us to create the DFS algorithm.

Stack data structure

A **stack** is a pile of objects placed one atop another (for example, a stack of books, a stack of clothes, or a stack of papers). There are two stacking operations: one for adding items to a stack, and one for removing items from a stack.

The operation used for adding items to a stack is called **push**, while the operation used for removing items is called as **pop**. Items are popped in the reverse order to push; that is why this data structure is called **last-in first-out** (**LIFO**).

Let's experiment with the stack data structure in Python. We'll be using the list data structure as a stack in Python. We'll use the `append()` method to push items to the stack and the `pop()` method to pop them out:

```
...
stack = []

print "stack", stack

#add items to the stack
stack.append(1)
stack.append(2)
stack.append(3)
stack.append(4)

print "stack", stack

#pop all the items out
while len(stack) > 0:
    item = stack.pop()
    print item
print "stack", stack
...
```

As shown in the preceding code, we have created an empty stack and we are printing it out. One by one, we are adding the numbers 1, 2, 3, and 4 to the stack and printing them out. Then, one by one, we are popping the items and printing them out; finally, we are printing the remaining stack.

If we execute the preceding code, `Stack.py`, we get the following output:

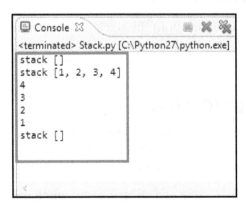

Figure 26

Initially, we have an empty stack, and when items 1, 2, 3, and 4 are pushed to the stack, we have 4 at the top of the stack. Now, when you pop the items out, the first one to come out is 4, then 3, then 2, and then 1; this is the reverse of the order of entry. Then, finally, we have an empty stack.

Now that we are clear on how stacks work, let's use these concepts to actually create a DFS algorithm.

The DFS algorithm

Now that you understand the basic concepts of searching, we'll look at how DFS works by using the three basic ingredients of search algorithms—the initial state, the successor function, and the goal function. We will use the stack data structure.

Let's first represent the DFS algorithm in the form of a flowchart, to offer a better understanding:

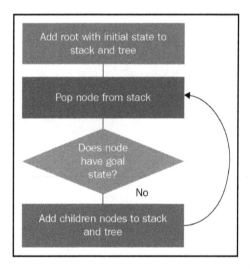

Figure 27

The steps in the preceding flowchart are as follows:

1. We create a root node using the initial state, and we add this to our stack and tree
2. We pop a node from the stack
3. We check whether it has the goal state; if it has the goal state, we stop our search here
4. If the answer to the condition in step 3 is **No**, then we find the child nodes of the pop node, and add them to the tree and stack
5. We repeat steps 2 to 4 until we either find the goal state or exhaust all of the nodes in the search tree

Let's apply the preceding algorithm to our filesystem, as follows:

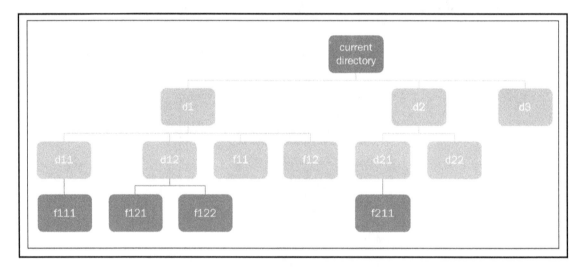

Figure 28

1. We create our root node, add it to the search tree, and add it to the stack. We pop a node from the stack, which is the **current directory** node.
2. The **current directory** node doesn't have the goal state, so we find its child nodes and add them to the tree and stack.

 When we add nodes to the stack, they have to be added in reverse order, so that the node on the top of the stack is on the leftmost side of the search tree.

3. We pop a node from the stack (**d1**); it doesn't have the goal state, so we find its child nodes and add it to the tree and stack.

4. We pop a node from the stack (**d11**); it doesn't have the goal state, so we find its child node, add it to the tree and stack.

5. We pop a node (**f111**); it doesn't have the goal state, and it also doesn't have child nodes, so we carry on.

6. We pop the next node, **d12**; we find its child nodes and add them to the tree and stack.

7. We pop the next node, **f121**, and it doesn't have any child nodes, so we carry on.

8. We pop the next node, **f122**, and it doesn't have any child nodes, so we carry on.

9. We pop the next node, **f11**, and we encounter the same case (where we have no child nodes), so we carry on; the same goes for **f12**.

10. We pop the next node, **d2**, and we find its child nodes and add them to the tree and stack.

11. We pop the next node, **d21**, and we find its child node and add it to the tree and stack.

12. We pop the next node, **f211**, and we find that it has the goal state, so we end our search here.

Let's try to implement these steps in code, as follows:

```
...
from Node import Node
from State import State


def performStackDFS():
    """
    This function performs DFS search using a stack
    """
    #create stack
    stack = []
    #create root node and add to stack
    initialState = State()
    root = Node(initialState)
    stack.append(root)
...
```

We have created a Python module called `StackDFS.py`, and it has a method called `performStackDFS()`. In this method, we have created an empty stack, which will hold all of our nodes, the `initialState`, a root node containing the `initialState`, and finally we have added this root node to the stack.

Remember that in `Stack.py`, we wrote a `while` loop to process all of the items in the stack. So, in the same way, in this case we will write a `while` loop to process all of the nodes in the stack:

```
. . .
while len(stack) > 0:
        #pop top node
        currentNode = stack.pop()
        print "-- pop --", currentNode.state.path
        #check if this is goal state
        if currentNode.state.checkGoalState():
            print "reached goal state"
            break
        #get the child nodes
        childStates = currentNode.state.successorFunction()
        for childState in childStates:
            childNode = Node(State(childState))
            currentNode.addChild(childNode)

    . . .
```

As shown in the preceding code, we pop the node from the top of the stack and call it `currentNode()`, and then we print it so that we can see the order in which the nodes are processed. We check whether the current node has the goal state, and if it does, we end our execution here. If it doesn't have the goal state, we find its child nodes and add it under `currentNode`, just like we did in `NodeTest.py`.

We will also add these child nodes to the stack, but in reverse order, using the following `for` loop:

```
...
for index in range(len(currentNode.children) - 1, -1, -1):
        stack.append(currentNode.children[index])

#print tree
    print "----------------------"
    root.printTree()
...
```

Finally, when we exit the `while` loop, we print the tree. Upon successful execution of the code, we will get the following output:

```
Console ⊠                                      ▣ ✖ ✖ ⚙ ▤ | ▤ ▤ ▤ | ▤ ⮌ ⮌ | ⮌ ▣ ▾ ▢ ▾ ▭ ▤
<terminated> StackDFS.py [C:\Python27\python.exe]
-- pop -- C:\Users\admin\Documents\9781787289376_Code\code\Section 1
-- pop -- C:\Users\admin\Documents\9781787289376_Code\code\Section 1\.project
-- pop -- C:\Users\admin\Documents\9781787289376_Code\code\Section 1\.pydevproject
-- pop -- C:\Users\admin\Documents\9781787289376_Code\code\Section 1\Do it yourself Code
-- pop -- C:\Users\admin\Documents\9781787289376_Code\code\Section 1\Do it yourself Code\Node.py
-- pop -- C:\Users\admin\Documents\9781787289376_Code\code\Section 1\Do it yourself Code\Node.pyc
-- pop -- C:\Users\admin\Documents\9781787289376_Code\code\Section 1\Do it yourself Code\RecursiveDFS.py
-- pop -- C:\Users\admin\Documents\9781787289376_Code\code\Section 1\Do it yourself Code\State.py
-- pop -- C:\Users\admin\Documents\9781787289376_Code\code\Section 1\Do it yourself Code\State.pyc
-- pop -- C:\Users\admin\Documents\9781787289376_Code\code\Section 1\Do it yourself Code\d1
-- pop -- C:\Users\admin\Documents\9781787289376_Code\code\Section 1\Do it yourself Code\d1\d11
-- pop -- C:\Users\admin\Documents\9781787289376_Code\code\Section 1\Do it yourself Code\d1\d11\f111.txt
-- pop -- C:\Users\admin\Documents\9781787289376_Code\code\Section 1\Do it yourself Code\d1\d12
-- pop -- C:\Users\admin\Documents\9781787289376_Code\code\Section 1\Do it yourself Code\d1\d12\f121.txt
-- pop -- C:\Users\admin\Documents\9781787289376_Code\code\Section 1\Do it yourself Code\d1\d12\f122.txt
-- pop -- C:\Users\admin\Documents\9781787289376_Code\code\Section 1\Do it yourself Code\d1\f11.txt
-- pop -- C:\Users\admin\Documents\9781787289376_Code\code\Section 1\Do it yourself Code\d1\f12.txt
-- pop -- C:\Users\admin\Documents\9781787289376_Code\code\Section 1\Do it yourself Code\d2
-- pop -- C:\Users\admin\Documents\9781787289376_Code\code\Section 1\Do it yourself Code\d2\d21
-- pop -- C:\Users\admin\Documents\9781787289376_Code\code\Section 1\Do it yourself Code\d2\d21\f211.txt
reached goal state
----------------------
```

Figure 29

The output displays the order in which the nodes are processed, and we can see the first node of the tree. Finally, we encounter our goal state, and our search stops:

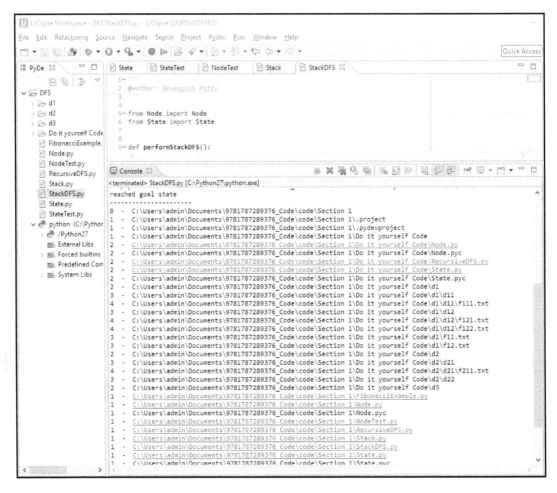

Figure 30

The preceding screenshot displays the search tree. Note that the preceding output and the one before it are almost the same. The only difference is that in the preceding screenshot, we can find two nodes, d22 and d3, because their parent nodes were explored.

Recursive DFS

When a function calls itself, we say that the function is a **recursive** function. Let's look at the example of the Fibonacci series. It is defined as follows: f(1) is equal to 1, f(2) is equal to 1, and for n greater than 2, f(n) is equal to f(n-1) + f(n-2). Let's look at the implementation of this function in code, as follows:

```
...
def fibonacci(n):
    if n <= 2:
        return 1
    else:
        return fibonacci(n-1) + fibonacci(n-2)

print "fibonacci(5)", fibonacci(5)
...
```

In the preceding code, we have created our function, fibonacci, which takes a number, n, as input. If n is less than or equal to 2, it returns 1; otherwise, it returns fibonacci(n-1) + fibonacci(n-2). Toward the end of the code, we have calculated the value of fibonacci(5), which is 5.

The output of running the preceding code is shown in the following screenshot:

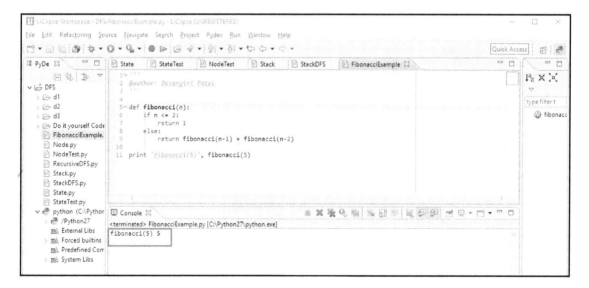

Figure 31

If we want to visualize the recursion tree of the `fibonacci` function, we can go to `https://visualgo.net/en/recursion`. This website has visualizations of various data structures and algorithms.

The visualization of a recursion tree is as follows:

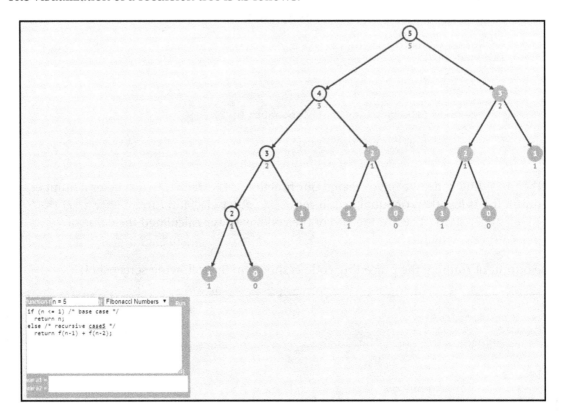

Figure 32

As shown in the preceding screenshot, the output that we get here is the same as the output we got with the code, and the order in which the nodes were explored is similar to DFS.

So, *what happens when function 1 calls function 2?* The program adds a stack frame to the program stack. A stack frame contains the local variables in function 1, the arguments passed to function 1, and the return addresses of function 2 and function 1.

Let's look at the example of the Fibonacci sequence again:

What Happens When a Function1 Calls a Function2?

```
def fibonacci (n):
    if n <= 2:
        return 1
    else:
        val1 = fibonacci (n-1)
        val2 = fibonacci (n-2)
        val = val1 + val2
        return val
```

Local variables = val1

Arguments passed = n

Return address = val2 ...

Figure 33

As you can see, the Fibonacci code has been modified for the sake of clarity. Suppose that the program is executing the line in bold, **val2 = fibonacci(n-2)**. Then, the stack frame created will contain the following values—local variables is equal to **val1**, arguments passed is equal to **n**, and return address is the address of the code in bold.

This means that the return address points to the unprocessed curve. Because in recursion the program stack keeps a stack of unprocessed calls, instead of storing nodes in the stack, we will call DFS recursively on the child nodes, so that the stack is indirectly maintained.

Let's look at the steps of recursive DFS in the following diagram:

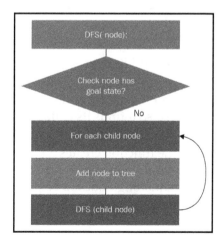

Figure 34

The steps in the preceding diagram are explained as follows:

1. We create an initial state.
2. We create a root node with this initial state.
3. We add the root node to the search tree and call DFS on the root node.
4. Recursive DFS is defined as follows: check whether the node has a goal state. If yes, then it returns the path; if no, then DFS finds the children node, and for each child node DFS adds the node to the tree, finally calling itself on the child node.

Now, we will apply the preceding algorithm to our filesystem, the steps for which are as follows:

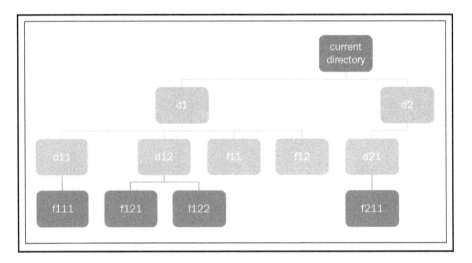

Figure 35

1. We create the root node and add it to the search tree, and we call DFS on this root node.
2. When we call DFS on this root node, the function checks whether this node has the goal state, and it doesn't, so it finds its children nodes (**d1**, **d2**, and **d3**). It takes the first node, **d1**, adds it to the search tree, and calls DFS on the node.
3. When it calls DFS on **d1**, the function creates a program. When DFS is called on **d1**, then the program creates a stack frame and adds it to the program stack. In this case, we'll show the remaining nodes to be processed in the `for` loop. Here, we're adding **d2** and **d3** in the program stack.

4. When DFS is called on **d1**, it finds the children nodes **d11**, **d12**, **f11**, and **f12**, and adds **d11** to the search tree.

5. It calls DFS on **d11**, and when it does so, it creates an entry in the program stack with the unprocessed nodes. Now, when DFS is called on **d11**, it finds the child node **f111**, adds **f111** to the search tree, and calls DFS on the node.

6. When DFS is called on **f111,** it has no children nodes, so it returns back; when this happens, the program stack is unwounded, which means that the program returns execution and processes the last unprocessed nodes in the stack. In this case, it starts processing node **d12**. So, the program adds node **d12** to the search tree, and calls DFS on **d1**.

7. When DFS is called on **d12**, it finds the children nodes **f121** and **f122**. It adds node **f121** to the search tree, and calls DFS on it. When DFS is called on **f121**, it adds the unprocessed node **f122** to the stack.

8. When DFS is called on **f121,** it has no children nodes, so again the stack is unwounded. So, we process node **f122**. This node is added to the search tree and DFS is called on it. So, we continue processing the last node, **f11**, add it to the search tree, and call DFS on it.

9. When we call DFS on **f11,** it has no children nodes, so again the stack is unwounded. We continue processing node **f12**, it is added to the search tree, and DFS is called on **f12**. We encounter this case, and we continue processing node **d2**. We add it to the search tree, and we call DFS on **d2**.

10. When we call DFS on **d2,** we find that is has children nodes: **d21** and **d22**. We add **d21** to the search tree, and we call DFS on **d21**; when we call DFS on **d21**, it creates an entry for **d22**. In the program stack, when DFS is called on **d21**, we find that it has a child, **f211**. This node is added to the search tree and DFS is called on **f211**.

11. When DFS is called an **f211**, we realize that it has the goal state, and we end our search process here.

Let's look at how we can implement recursive DFS, as follows:

```
...
from State import State
from Node import Node


class RecursiveDFS():
    """
    This performs DFS search
    """
    def __init__(self):
```

```
        self.found = False
    ...
```

As shown in the preceding code, we have created a Python module called `RecursiveDFS.py`. It has a class called `RecursiveDFS`, and, in the constructor, it has a property called `found`, which indicates whether the solution has been found. We'll look at the significance of the `found` variable later.

Let's look at the following lines of code:

```
    ...
    def search(self):
        """
        This method performs the search
        """
        #get the initial state
        initialState = State()
        #create root node
        rootNode = Node(initialState)
        #perform search from root node
        self.DFS(rootNode)
        rootNode.printTree()
    ...
```

Here, we have a method called `search`, in which we are creating the `initialState`, and the `rootNode` we're calling the DFS function on the `rootNode`. Finally, we print the tree after we perform the DFS search, as follows:

```
    ...
    def DFS(self, node):
        """
        This creates the search tree
        """
        if not self.found:
            print "-- proc --", node.state.path
            #check if we have reached goal state
            if node.state.checkGoalState():
                print "reached goal state"
                #self.found = True
            else:
                #find the successor states from current state
                childStates = node.state.successorFunction()
                #add these states as children nodes of current node
                for childState in childStates:
                    childNode = Node(State(childState))
                    node.addChild(childNode)
```

```
self.DFS(childNode)
```

. . . .

The `DFS` function can be defined as follows:

- If the solution has not been found, then the node that is being processed is printed
- We check whether the node has the goal state, and if it does, we print that the goal state has been reached
- If it doesn't have the goal state, we find the child states; next, we create the child node for each child state, we add them to the tree, and we call `DFS` on each of the child nodes

Let's execute the program; we will get the following output:

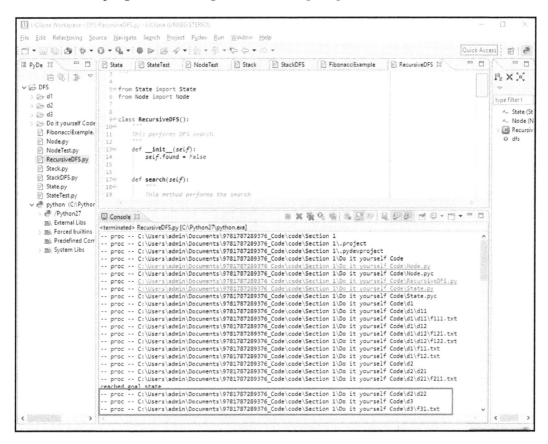

Figure 36

When we processed f211, we reached the goal state, but here we have three extra lines; this is because these nodes have been added to the program stack. To remove these lines, we have created a variable called found, so that when the goal state is found, the variable will be set to True. Once we encounter f211, the remaining nodes in the program stack will not be processed:

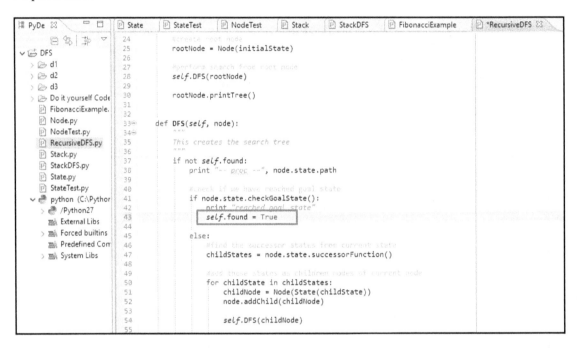

Figure 37

Let's run this code again and see what happens:

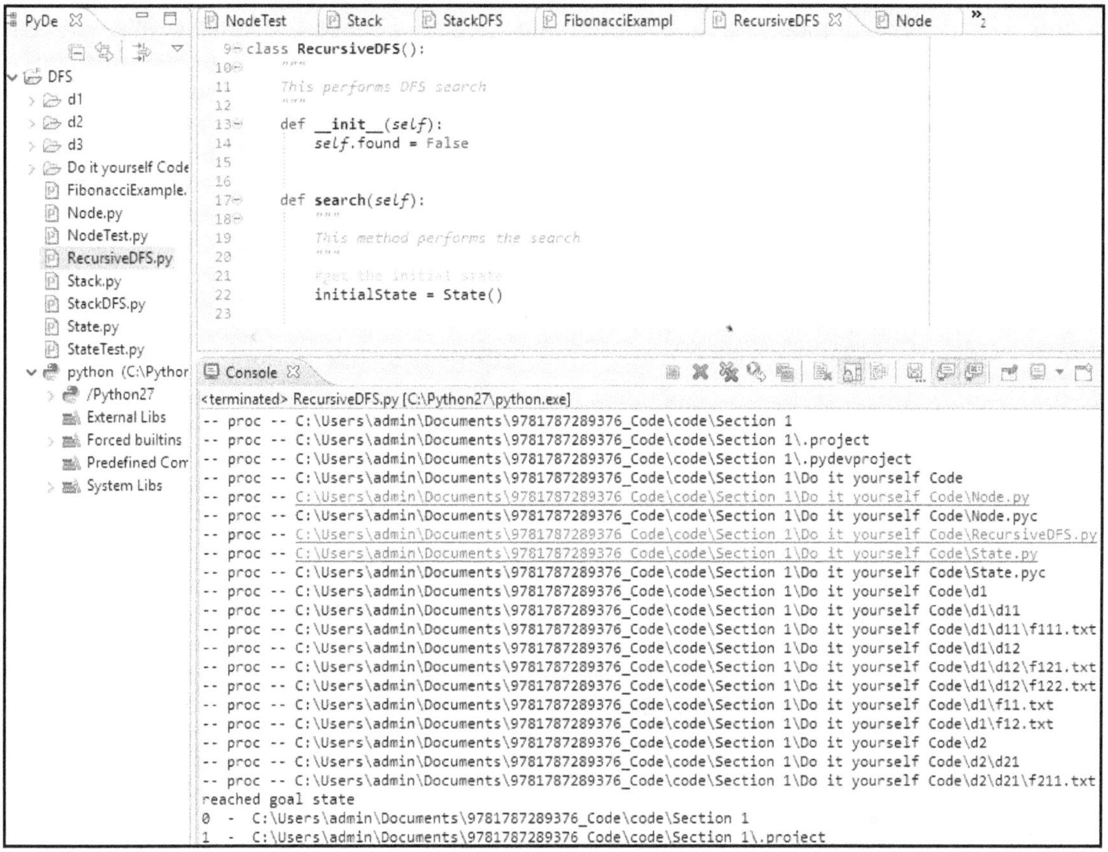

Figure 38

As you can see, once we've processed `f211` and reached the goal state, the node processing stops. The output of the `printTree` function is the same as what we store in `StackDFS.py`.

Now that you understand how DFS can be made into a recursive function, in the next topic we will look at an application that you can develop by yourself.

Do it yourself

In this section, we will look at an application that you can develop by yourself. We will take a look at a new application and discuss the changes that are required. In the *Introduction to file search applications* section, we discussed two applications of file searching; now, we will develop the second type of example. Our aim is to develop a search application that is able to find program files containing specific program text.

In the code for recursive DFS, we mainly used three classes, as follows:

- **State**: This has the three main ingredients of the search process
- **Node**: This is used to build search trees
- **Recursive DFS**: This has the actual algorithm implementation

Suppose that we want to adapt this code or file search application to new application. We will need to change three methods: `getInitialState`, `successorFunction`, and `checkGoalState`. For the new application of program searching, you will need to change just one method: `checkGoalState`.

In your new `checkGoalState` function, you will need to open the file, read the contents of the file line by line, and perform a substring check or regular expression check. Lastly, based on the results of the check, you will return true or false.

So, go ahead and try it out for yourself!

Summary

In this chapter, we looked at four basic concepts related to searching: the state, which is the condition of our search process; the node, which is used for building a search tree; the stack, which helps to traverse the search tree and decides the order in which the nodes are traversed; and recursion, which eliminates the need for an explicit stack. You also learned about DFS, which explores the search tree in a depth-first order.

In the next chapter, you'll learn about **breadth-first search** (**BFS**), which explores a search tree in a breadth-first order. See you there!

 Please refer to the link `https://www.packtpub.com/sites/default/files/downloads/HandsOnArtificialIntelligenceforSearch_ColorImages.pdf` for the colored images of this chapter.

2
Understanding the Breadth-First Search Algorithm

The **breadth-first search** (**BFS**) algorithm is a traversing algorithm where you start at a selected node (the source or starting node) and traverse the graph layer-wise, exploring the neighboring nodes (nodes that are directly connected to the source node). You then move towards the neighboring nodes in the next level.

In this chapter, you will learn about BFS while developing LinkedIn's connection feature. You will learn how second-degree connections can be computed by using the BFS algorithm.

In this chapter, we will cover the following topics:

- Understanding the LinkedIn connection feature
- Graph data structure
- Queue data structure
- The BFS algorithm
- DFS versus BFS

Understanding the LinkedIn connection feature

As you know, LinkedIn is a social network, and users are connected to one another through first- or second-degree connections. In order to better understand this concept, use the following diagram as a reference:

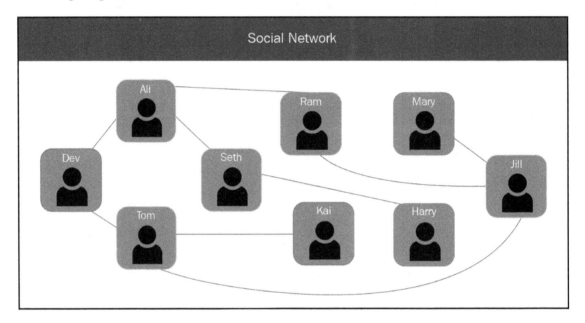

Figure 1

Suppose that I want to find an acquaintance named **Jill** and connect with her. When I go to her profile, I find that she is a second-degree connection, which means that we have a mutual colleague. Let's look at how this degree is computed. To do so, we will create a connection tree:

1. We start with the profile node, **Dev**, and add it to the connection tree:

Figure 2

2. Now, I will find my colleagues and add them beneath my node. So, I add **Ali** and **Tom** beneath the **Dev** node:

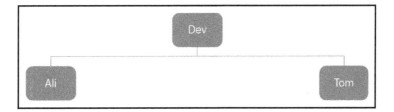

Figure 3

3. Now, for both **Ali** and **Tom**, I find their colleagues and add them beneath their nodes. So, under **Ali**, I add **Dev**, **Seth**, and **Ram**, and under **Tom,** I add **Dev**, **Seth**, **Kai**, and **Jill**:

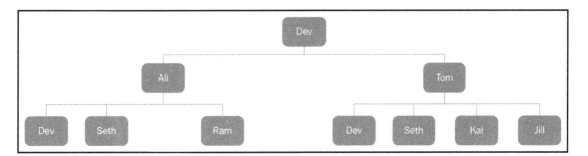

Figure 4

4. Now, for each of these nodes, we find their connections and add those as well:

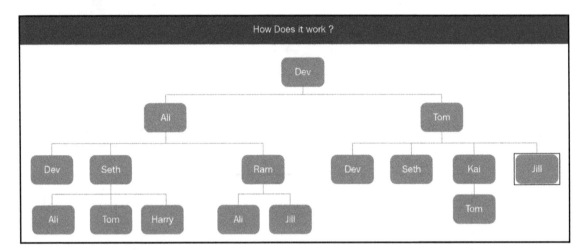

Figure 5

In the preceding diagram, the connections to **Dev** have been added (due to space constraints, this is not shown). For **Seth**, we find his connections (**Ali**, **Tom**, and **Harry**) and add them underneath his name. For **Ram**, we add **Ali** and **Jill**. Similarly, due to space constraints, we are not showing the connections for **Dev** and **Seth**, as they are already shown in the diagram. Under **Kai**, we add his connection, **Tom**. Finally, when we come to the node for **Jill** (to add her connections), we find that this node has the goal state, so we end our search.

You may have noticed that **Jill** appears as a connection to **Ram** at the bottom of the tree; but, if you consider the bottom node, then the connection degree is **3**, which is not the least value. However, because a BFS search processes the search tree level by level, we're able to find the least path solution. We can also see that there are people that appear multiple times in this connection tree. For example, **Dev**, **Ali**, and **Tom** appear three times each, while **Seth** and **Jill** each appear twice.

So, we'll keep the first entry of the node in the connection tree, and we will remove the other instances; the following diagram shows how the search tree should look:

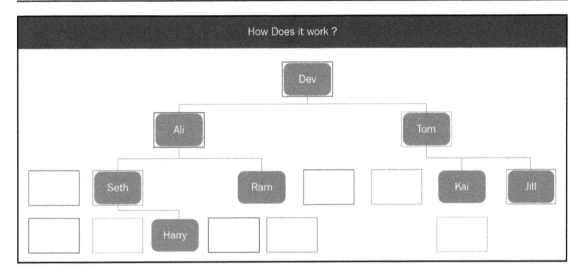

Figure 6

When we add the node to the search tree, we should check whether it already exists in the search tree.

In Chapter 1, *Understanding the Depth-First Search Algorithm,* you learned that the State class indicates the condition of the search process. You also learned that the State class has to be changed for every application, even though the search algorithm is the same. Now, let's look at the changes that we need to make to the State class for this application.

First, we need a property to track the condition of the search. In this case, the property is the person under consideration. Then, we have the same four methods—constructor(), getInitialState(), successorFunction(), and checkGoalState().

Let's look at each of these three ingredients in detail. To find the initial state, we should ask ourselves the question, *where do we start searching from?* In this application, we start searching from my profile. To find the successor function, we should ask ourselves, *how do we explore from the current state?* In this application, the function should return the people connected to the person under consideration. So, for **Ali** it should return all of his colleagues. Finally, to find the goal function, we should ask the question, *how will we know when we have found the solution?* The goal function should return true if the person is Jill. So, if the current person is Harry, the function should return false, and if the current person is Jill, it should return true.

Let's look at the `State` class code for this application, as follows:

```python
. . .
from GraphData import *
class State:
    '''
    This class retrieves state information for social connection
    feature
    '''
    def __init__(self, name = None):
        if name == None:
            #create initial state
            self.name = self.getInitialState()
        else:
            self.name = name
    def getInitialState(self):
        """
        This method returns me.
        """
        initialState = "Dev"
        return initialState
    def successorFunction(self):
        """
        This is the successor function. It finds all the persons
        connected to the current person
        """
        return connections[self.name]
. . .
```

As shown in the preceding code, in this module, `State.py`, we are importing all of the variables from `GraphData`. The purpose of `GraphData` will be explained in the *Graph data structure* section. In the constructor, the `name` argument is passed. If the argument `name` is `None`, then the initial state is created, and if the name is provided, that name is assigned to the name property. The `initialState` property holds the value `Dev`, and the `successorFunction` method returns all of the people connected to the current person. To get the people connected to the person, we use connections from GraphData:

```python
    def checkGoalState(self):
        """
        This method checks whether the person is Jill.
        """
        #check if the person's name is Jill
        return self.name == "Jill"
```

The `checkGoalState` function returns if the current person's name is `Jill`.

Now, you should understand how the degree of connection is computed and how the `State` class has changed for this application.

In the next section, we'll look at how to represent social network data as a graph.

Graph data structure

A **graph** is a non-linear data structure containing a set of points known as **nodes** (or vertices) and a set of links known as **edges**, as illustrated in the following diagram:

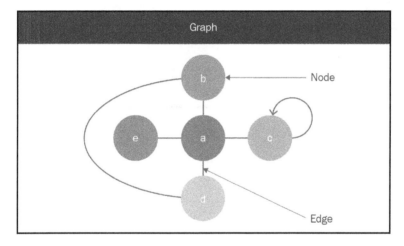

Figure 7

An edge that connects to the same node is called a **cycle**. As shown in the preceding diagram, nodes **a** and **b** are connected by two paths; one is through edge **a-b**, and the other is through edges **a-d** and **d-b**. A **tree** is a special type of graph, in which there are no cycles, and two nodes are connected by one path.

In Python, we can use a dictionary structure to represent a graph. A **dictionary** is a data structure where many keys are mapped to values. For a dictionary that represents a graph, the keys are the nodes, and the values of those nodes are the nodes that they are connected to:

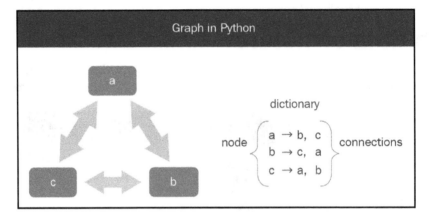

Figure 8

In the preceding diagram, we can see that the following applies:

- **For key a**, the values are **b** and **c**
- **For key b**, the values are **c** and **a**
- **For key c**, the values are **a** and **b**

Now, let's create a dictionary to show the graph structure of the social network that we saw in the previous topic:

```
...
#create a dictionary with all the mappings
connections = {}
connections["Dev"] = {"Ali", "Seth", "Tom"}
connections["Ali"] = {"Dev", "Seth", "Ram"}
connections["Seth"] = {"Ali", "Tom", "Harry"}
connections["Tom"] = {"Dev", "Seth", "Kai", 'Jill'}
connections["Ram"] = {"Ali", "Jill"}
connections["Kai"] = {"Tom"}
connections["Mary"] = {"Jill"}
connections["Harry"] = {"Seth"}
connections["Jill"] = {"Ram", "Tom", "Mary"}
...
```

In the Python module `GraphData.py`, we have created a dictionary called `connections`. The keys are the people in the social network, and the corresponding values are the people that they are connected to. Now, the `connections` dictionary is used in `State.py`. It is used in the `successorFunction` function, as shown in the following code:

```
...
def successorFunction(self):
        """
        This is the successor function. It finds all the persons
        connected to the current person
        """
        return connections[self.name]
...
```

Here, we can get the people that the person is connected to by using the `connections` dictionary, with the person's name as the key. We can get the people that are connected to that person by using the `connections` object.

Now, let's look at how to traverse this graph data structure, in order to create a search tree:

1. We will start with my profile in the graph, and add the **Dev** node to the search tree and the visited nodes list.
2. From my node in the graph, we can find the connected people, **Ali** and **Tom**; we add these nodes to the search tree and the visited nodes list.
3. For **Ali** and **Tom**, we find who they're connected to by using the graph data structure, and we add these nodes to the search tree and the visited nodes list, if they have not been visited before. **Ali** is connected to **Dev**, **Seth**, and **Ram**. **Dev** has already been visited, so we ignore this node. **Seth** and **Ram** have not been visited before, so we add these nodes to the search tree and the visited nodes list. **Tom** is connected to **Dev**, **Seth**, **Kai**, and **Jill**. **Dev** and **Seth** have already been visited, so we ignore these nodes, and we add the nodes **Kai** and **Jill** to the list, because they have not been visited before.
4. We repeat the process of adding the children to the search tree and the visited nodes list (if they have not been visited before). **Seth** is connected to **Ali**, **Tom**, and **Harry**. **Ali** and **Tom** have already been visited, so we ignore them, and we add **Harry** to the search tree and the visited nodes list. **Ram** is connected to **Ali** and **Jill**, and both of them have been visited before. Moving forward, **Kai** is connected to **Tom**, and he's already been visited, as well. When we process the **Jill** node, we find that it has the goal state, and we end our search.

You have now learned how to use a list of visited nodes to explore a graph as a tree, which will look like the following:

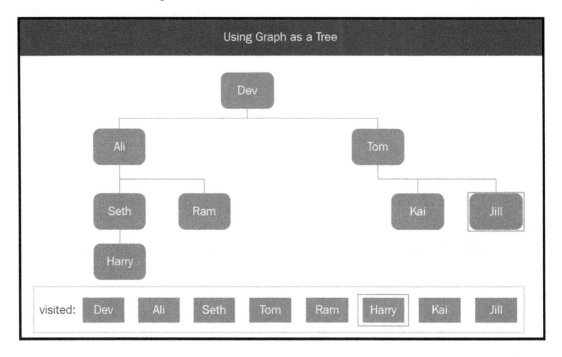

Figure 9

In the next section, you'll learn about the queue data structure, which forms the basis of node reversal, just like a stack in the DFS method.

Queue data structure

A **queue** is a sequence of people or objects waiting to be attended to. Some examples include a queue of people waiting at a counter, a queue of swimmers that are ready to dive in to a pool, and a queue of songs in a playlist:

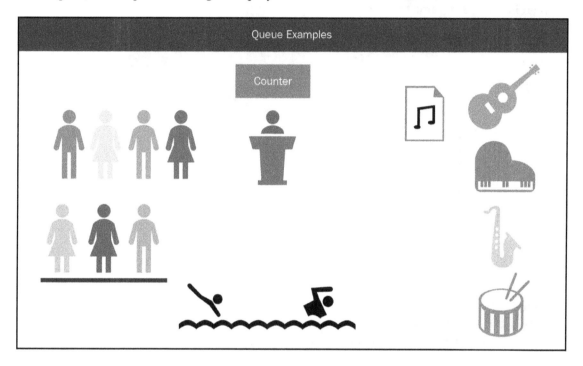

Figure 10

Just like in a stack, there are two types of operations—one for inserting items into a queue, and one for removing items from a queue. When a person joins a queue, he or she must stand behind the last person. The operation of adding an item to a queue is called **enqueue**. The first person to be attended to in a queue is the person standing in the front. The operation to remove an item from a queue is called **dequeue**. Queue operations can be seen in the following diagram:

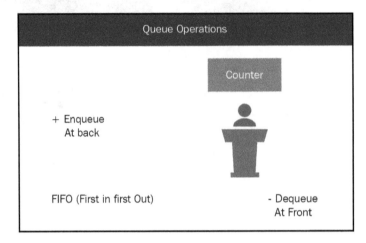

Figure 11

Since the first object inserted is the first one to be removed, this data structure is called **first in first out (FIFO)**. In Python, we can use the deque class to create queue objects.
The deque class provides two methods—one method, append, for inserting items, and a method called popleft for removing items:

```
...
from collections import deque

queue = deque([])
print queue

queue.append("1")
queue.append("2")
queue.append("3")
queue.append("4")

print queue
...
```

In the preceding code, we have created an empty queue, to which we will add the items 1, 2, 3, and 4; later, we will delete these items from the queue one by one. Upon successful execution of the code, we will get the following output:

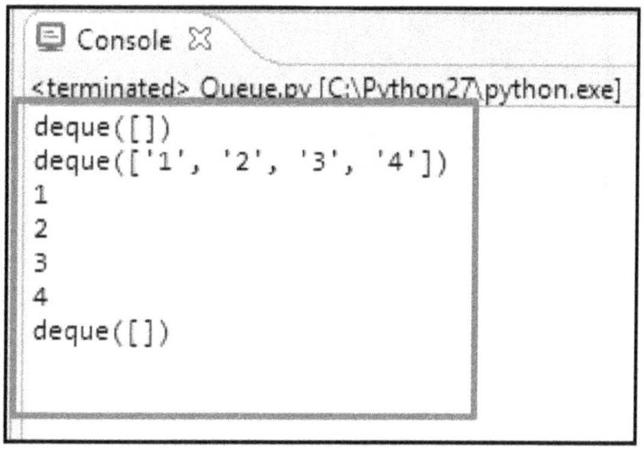

```
Console  ☒
<terminated> Queue.py [C:\Python27\python.exe]
deque([])
deque(['1', '2', '3', '4'])
1
2
3
4
deque([])
```

Figure 12

As shown in the preceding screenshot, we initially have an empty queue, and, after adding items 1, 2, 3, and 4, you can see that the items are in the queue, with 1 at the front and 4 at the back. When we remove an item from the queue, the first one to be removed is 1, because it is at the front, and then 2, 3, and 4 are removed. At the end, we have an empty queue.

Now that you understand how a queue works, we'll look at the steps in a BFS algorithm and how the graph and queue data structures are used.

The BFS algorithm

In this section, we'll look at the flow of the BFS algorithm, how a queue is used, and how graph data affects the algorithm. The flow of the BFS algorithm is similar to that of DFS, but instead of using a stack data structure, a queue data structure is used.

A flowchart of the BFS algorithm can be illustrated as follows:

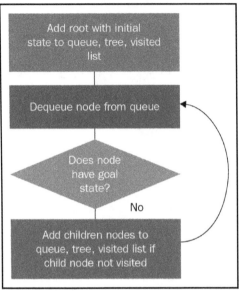

Figure 13

1. We initially create a root node with an initial state, and add it to a queue and tree.
2. A node is dequeued from the queue, and we check whether it has the goal state. If it does, we end our search. If it doesn't, we find the child nodes of the dequeued node and add them to the queue entry.
3. This process is repeated until we either find the goal state or have exhausted all of the nodes in our search tree.
4. Since our connection data is in a graph structure, we have to check whether each node has been visited before.
5. So, we add the root node to a list of visited nodes, and the child node is added to the queue, tree, and visited list (if the child node has not been visited previously).

Let's look at these steps in detail by implementing them in our graph diagram, which we covered in the *Understanding the LinkedIn connection feature* section:

1. We start by adding my profile node to the search tree, queue, and visited nodes list. We dequeue the **Dev** node from the queue.

2. Since the **Ali** node has not been visited, we add this node to the search tree, queue, and visited nodes list. Similarly, since **Tom** has not been visited, we add this node to the search tree, queue, and visited nodes list.

3. We dequeue the **Ali** node from the queue, and, since it doesn't have the goal state, we find its child nodes: **Dev**, **Seth,** and **Ram**. The **Dev** node has been visited, so we ignore that node. The **Seth** node has not been visited, so we add that node to the search tree, queue, and visited nodes list. Similarly, we add **Ram** to the search tree, queue, and visited nodes list.

4. We dequeue the **Tom** node from the queue, and we find its children nodes: **Dev**, **Seth, Kai,** and **Jill**. The **Dev** node has been visited, so we ignore that node, and the same goes for the **Seth** node. The **Kai** node has not been visited, so we add that node to the search tree, queue, and visited nodes list; the same goes for the **Jill** node. We dequeue the **Seth** node from the queue, and we find its child nodes: **Ali**, **Tom**, and **Harry**. The **Ali** and **Tom** nodes have been visited, so we ignore these nodes. We add the node **Harry** to the search tree, queue, and visited nodes list.

5. We dequeue the **Ram** node from the queue, and we find its child nodes, **Ali** and **Jill**, which have both been visited; so, we carry on.

6. We dequeue the **Kai** node, and we find its child node, **Tom**, which has been visited; so, we carry on again.

7. We dequeue the **Jill** node from the queue, and we find that it has the goal state, so we end our search.

Once we have completed the preceding steps, we will have the following tree:

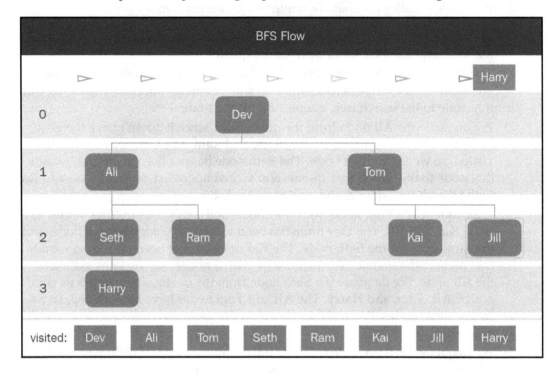

Figure 14

Let's implement the preceding algorithm with the following code:

```
...
def performQueueBFS():
    """
    This function performs BFS search using a queue
    """
    #create queue
    queue = deque([])
    #since it is a graph, we create visited list
    visited = []
    #create root node
    initialState = State()
    root = Node(initialState)
    #add to queue and visited list
    queue.append(root)
    visited.append(root.state.name)
...
```

In the Python module `QueueBFS.py`, we have created a method called `performQueueBFS`, in which we have an empty queue that will hold the nodes and a list of visited nodes. We create the root node with `initialState`, and we add this root node to the queue, along with a list of visited nodes. One by one, we dequeue elements from the queue; we call the dequeued node the `currentNode`:

```
. . .
            while len(queue) > 0:
            #get first item in queue
            currentNode = queue.popleft()
            print "-- dequeue --", currentNode.state.name
            #check if this is goal state
            if currentNode.state.checkGoalState():
                print "reached goal state"
                #print the path
                print "---------------------"
                print "Path"
                currentNode.printPath()
                break
. . .
```

We print the name of the current node and check whether it has the goal state. If it does, we print the path from the root node to the current node and break the loop. If it doesn't have the goal state, we find the child states of the current state, and for each higher state, we construct the child node and check whether that node has been visited.

The list of visited nodes now holds the names of the nodes. So, in the following code, we have added the name of the root node:

```
visited.append(root.state.name)
```

We have done the same in the following code:

```
. . .
#check if node is not visited
            if childNode.state.name not in visited:
                #add this node to visited nodes
                visited.append(childNode.state.name)
                #add to tree and queue
                currentNode.addChild(childNode)
                queue.append(childNode)
    #print tree
    print "---------------------"
    print "Tree"
    root.printTree()
. . .
```

In the preceding code, we check whether the name of the node has not been visited. Because we're checking for unique names, if the node has not been visited, we add the name of the child node to the list of visited nodes, and we add the child node to the search tree and the queue. Finally, we print the queue.

Let's run the code and see what happens:

Figure 15

In the preceding screenshot, we can see the order in which the nodes are processed. We start off with the Dev node, and then we process the connections, Ali and Tom, and then the connections of Ali, Ram, and Seth, and the connections of Tom, Kai and Jill. When we process the Jill node, we find that we have reached the goal state and we end our search.

In the preceding screenshot, we can see the path printed from the initial state to the goal state through the `Tom` node . From this, we can see that `Jill` is a second-level connection. We can also see the search tree that has been constructed so far.

Now that you are aware of the steps involved in BFS, we'll compare the BFS and DFS algorithms.

BFS versus DFS

In this section, we'll look at the differences between the DFS and BFS algorithms. We will compare these differences in terms of various factors.

Order of traversal

In DFS, preference is given to child nodes, which means that after node **a** and node **b** are explored, and after node **b** and node **c** are explored, we hit a dead end and we backtrack to the previous level. This means that we go back to node **b,** and then to its next child, which is node **c**.

In BFS, the nodes are covered level by level, and preference is given to siblings. This means that after node **a**, nodes **b** and **e** are explored, and after that, nodes **c**, **d**, and **f** are explored, as indicated by the following diagram:

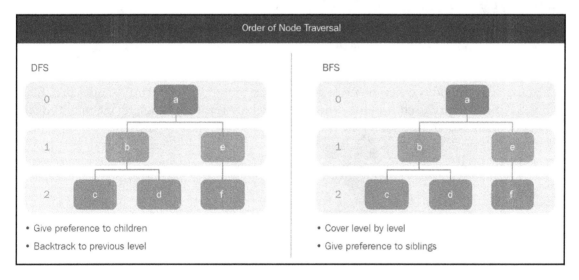

Figure 16

Data structures

In DFS, a stack data structure is used, while in BFS, a queue is used, as shown in the following diagram:

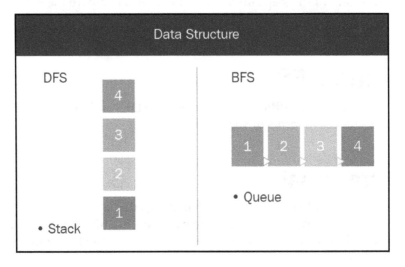

Figure 17

Memory

When recursive DFS is called on node **c**, the implicit stack stores two entries—one for node **e**, and one for nodes **c** and **d**. So, the memory used is in the order of **d**, where **d** is the depth of the search tree.

When the BFS method is called on node **c**, the queue contains four entries—nodes **c**, **d**, **f**, and **g**. So, the memory used is in the order of $b^\wedge d$, where **b** is the branching factor and **d** is the depth of the search tree. Here, the branching factor is **2**, because each internal node has two children:

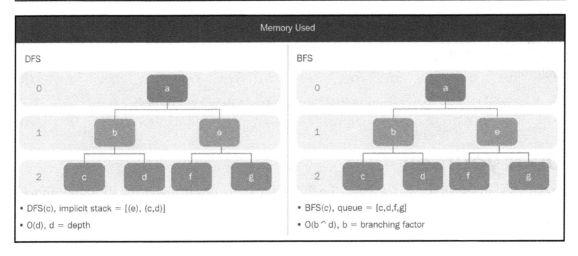

Figure 18

Optimal solution

Suppose that there are two possible solutions—nodes **d** and **e**. In this case, **e** is the optimal solution, because it has the shortest path from root node **a**. Here, DFS finds the sub-optimal solution, **d**, before it finds the optimal solution, **e**. BFS finds the optimal solution, **e,** before it encounters node **d**:

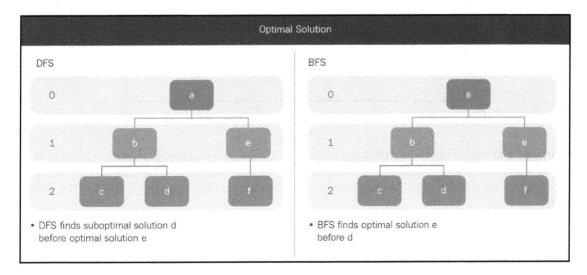

Figure 19

We already saw that DFS uses less memory than BFS, and BFS finds the optimal solution. So, the choice of algorithm depends on how big the search space is (in this case, you will go for DFS), and whether finding the optimal solution is important (in this case, BFS is preferred).

Next, we will look at an application that you can try to develop yourself.

Do it yourself

In the previous section, we discussed the differences between the DFS and BFS algorithms. In this section, we'll look at an application that you can try to develop yourself. We'll go over the application that you'll try to develop, and the changes that are required for the application.

Your aim will be to develop a university navigation application, as shown in the following diagram:

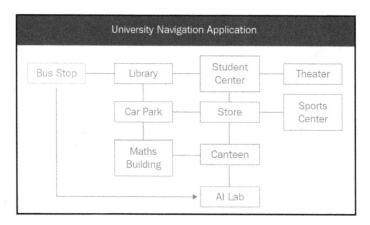

Figure 20

Suppose that this is the layout of the university, and people can travel along horizontal or vertical lines. In this application, the user has to enter the source and destination places. For this specific case, we'll assume that a new student wants to find his way from the **Bus Stop** to the **AI Lab**.

You can refer to the classes that we developed for the LinkedIn connection feature, as follows:

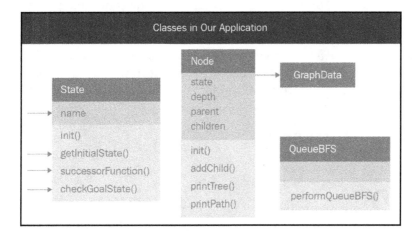

Figure 21

To adapt that code for this application, we need to change the State class and the graph data. In the State class, the name property is replaced with the place property, and NavigationData contains the connections between places:

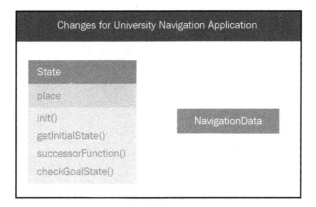

Figure 22

Let's look at the three ingredients of the search in detail. To get the answer for the initial state, we can ask ourselves the question, *where do we start searching from?* In this case, it's the **Bus Stop**. So, `successorFunction` should return all of the connected places. For example, if the current place is **Car Park**, then this function should return the **Library**, the **Store**, and the **Maths Building**. To get the answer for the goal function, we should ask ourselves the question, *how will we know when we have found the solution?* For this application, the function should return true if the place is the **AI Lab**; for example, if the current place is the **Canteen**, then it should return false, and if the current place is the **AI Lab**, then it should return true.

Go ahead and try it out for yourself!

Summary

In this chapter, to help you understand the BFS algorithm, we revisited the concepts of state and node. You learned about the graph and queue data structures, and we discussed the differences between the DFS and BFS algorithms.

In the next chapter, you'll be learning about the heuristic search algorithm. Instead of giving preference to child or sibling nodes, this method gives preference to the nodes that are closest to the goal state; the term **heuristic** refers to the measure of how close the nodes are to the goal state.

Please refer to the link
`https://www.packtpub.com/sites/default/files/downloads/HandsOnAr`
`tificialIntelligenceforSearch_ColorImages.pdf` for the colored images of this chapter.

3
Understanding the Heuristic Search Algorithm

Heuristic searching is an AI search technique that utilizes a heuristic for its functionality. A **heuristic** is a general guideline that most likely prompts an answer. Heuristics assume a noteworthy role in searching strategies, in view of the exponential nature of most problems. Heuristics help to decrease a high quantity of options from an exponential number to a polynomial number. In **artificial intelligence (AI)**, heuristic searching is of general significance, and also has specific importance. In a general sense, the term heuristic is utilized for any exercise that is regularly successful, but isn't certain to work in every situation. In heuristic search design, the term heuristic often alludes to the extraordinary instance of a heuristic evaluation function.

In this chapter, we will cover the following topics:

- Revisiting the navigation application
- The priority queue data structure
- Visualizing search trees
- Greedy **Best-First Search (BFS)**
- The A* Search
- Features of a good heuristic

Revisiting the navigation application

In Chapter 2, *Understanding the Breadth-First Search Algorithm*, we saw the university navigation application, with which we wanted to find our way from the Bus Stop to the AI Lab. In the BFS method, we assume that the distance between connected places is one (that is, the same). However, in reality, that is not the case. Now, let's assume that the university is designed as follows:

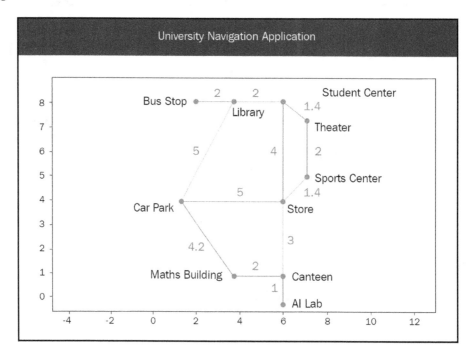

Figure 1

The values in green are the actual distances between the connected places. Let's go ahead and create a dictionary, storing the locations of these places:

```
...
#connections between places
connections = {}
connections["Bus Stop"] = {"Library"}
connections["Library"] = {"Bus Stop", "Car Park", "Student Center"}
connections["Car Park"] = {"Library", "Maths Building", "Store"}
connections["Maths Building"] = {"Car Park", "Canteen"}
connections["Student Center"] = {"Library", "Store" , "Theater"}
connections["Store"] = {"Student Center", "Car Park", "Canteen", "Sports
Center"}
```

```
connections["Canteen"] = {"Maths Building", "Store", "AI Lab"}
connections["AI Lab"] = {"Canteen"}
connections["Theater"] = {"Student Center", "Sports Center"}
connections["Sports Center"] = {"Theater", "Store"}
...
```

In the Python `NavigationData.py` module, we have created a dictionary called `connections`; this dictionary stores the connections between places. They are similar to the connections between people that we saw in the LinkedIn connection feature application in `Chapter 2`, *Understanding the Breadth-First Search Algorithm*:

```
...
#location of all the places

location = {}
location["Bus Stop"] = [2, 8]
location["Library"] = [4, 8]
location["Car Park"] = [1, 4]
location["Maths Building"] = [4, 1]
location["Student Center"] = [6, 8]
location["Store"] = [6, 4]
location["Canteen"] = [6, 1]
location["AI Lab"] = [6, 0]
location["Theater"] = [7, 7]
location["Sports Center"] = [7, 5]
...
```

We also have the `location` dictionary for storing the locations of places. The keys of the `location` dictionary are the places, and the values are the x and y coordinates of those places.

In DFS, preference was given to the child nodes while exploring the search tree; in BFS, preference was given to the sibling nodes. In heuristic searching, preference is given to nodes with lower heuristic values.

Now, let's look at the term *heuristic*. A heuristic is a property of the class node. It is a guess, or estimate, of which node will lead to the goal state faster than others. This is a strategy used to reduce the nodes explored and reach the goal state quicker:

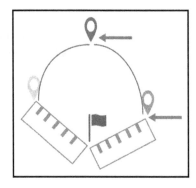

Figure 2

For example, suppose that we're at the red node in the preceding diagram, and it has two child nodes—the yellow node and the green node. The green node seems to be much closer to the goal state, so we would select that node for further exploration.

We'll see the following two heuristic search algorithms as we proceed with this chapter:

- The greedy BFS algorithm
- The A* Search algorithm

The priority queue data structure

A **priority queue** is a queue in which each element has a priority. For example, when passengers are waiting in a queue to board a flight, families with young children and business class passengers usually take priority and board first; then, the economy class passengers board. Let's look at another example. Suppose that three people are waiting in a queue to be attended to at a service counter, and an old man steps in at the end of the queue. Considering his age, the people in the queue might give him a higher priority and allow him to go first. Through these two examples, we can see that the elements in a priority queue have priorities, and they are processed in order of those priorities.

Just like in queuing, we have operations to insert elements into a priority queue. The **insert** operation inserts an element with a specific priority. Consider the following diagram, illustrating the insert operation:

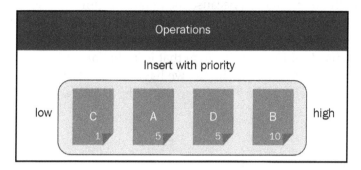

Figure 3

In the preceding diagram, element **A** is inserted with priority **5**; since the priority queue is empty, the element is kept at the front. In Python, elements with low priorities are arranged toward the front of the queue, and elements with high priority values are arranged toward the end of the priority queue. This means that elements with low priority values are processed first, since they're at the front of the priority queue. Now, suppose that element **B** needs to be inserted with priority **10**. As **10** is greater than **5**, element **B** is kept after element **A**. Now, suppose that element **C** is to be inserted with priority **1**. Because **1** is less than **5**, it is arranged in front of element **A**. Next, element **D** is to be inserted with priority **5**; here, both elements **A** and **D** have priority **5**, but, since **A** was inserted first, it has a higher priority. This means that **D** is placed after **A** and before **B**.

In a queue, we have an operation called **dequeue**, which removes an element from the front. Similarly, in a priority queue, we have an operation called **get front element**, which removes an element from the front of the priority queue. So, calling this operation four times should first remove **C**, then **A**, then **D**, and finally **B**.

In Python, we have the `Queue` class for the priority queue data structure. It has the `PriorityQueue` method, which takes `maxsize` as an argument for creating a priority queue. If `maxsize` is less than 0 or equal to 0, the queue size is infinite. In our case, we'll call this method with no arguments, because the default argument is 0. In `PriorityQueue`, the elements of the tuple are `priority_number` and `data`. The `Queue` class has the `empty()` method, which returns `True` if it's empty and `False` otherwise. It has the `put()` method, used for inserting an item that is in the form of a tuple: `(priority_number, data)`. Finally, we have the `get()` method, which returns the front element. Let's go ahead and try out these methods, as follows:

```
...
import Queue

pqueue = Queue.PriorityQueue()
print pqueue.qsize()

pqueue.put((5, 'A'))
pqueue.put((10, 'B'))
pqueue.put((1, 'C'))
pqueue.put((5, 'D'))

print pqueue.qsize()

while not pqueue.empty():
    print pqueue.get()
print pqueue.qsize()
...
```

We have created a Python module called `PriorityQueue.py`, and we are importing the `Queue` class. We have also created a priority queue and, one by one, we are inserting elements with specific priorities.

As can be seen in the preceding code, we are inserting a tuple where the priority number is 5 and the data is A; then, we are inserting element B with priority 10, C with priority 1, and D with priority 5. We are also checking whether the priority queue is empty and when it is not empty, we are printing all of the elements one by one, as follows:

```
Console ⊠
<terminated> PriorityQueue.py [C:\Python27\python.exe]
0
4
(1, 'C')
(5, 'A')
(5, 'D')
(10, 'B')
0
```

Figure 4

As you can see, in the preceding output, the priority queue is initially empty. After inserting the four elements, the length becomes 4; when we get the front elements, the first element is C, the next is A, the next is D, and the last element is B.

Visualizing a search tree

In the previous chapter, you learned that a **graph** is a structure in which nodes are connected by edges. A **tree** is a special type of graph, in which there are no cycles and two nodes are connected by one path. For visualizing trees, we'll use the pydot Python library, which is a Python interface to Graphviz's DOT language. In Chapter 1, *Understanding the Depth-First Search Algorithm*, we learned that **Graphviz** is open source graph visualization software, and it provides the DOT language for creating layered drawings of directed graphs. In addition, we'll be using the matplotlib library for displaying the final rendered image.

Now, let's use these libraries to visualize the following simple tree. It has a root node, and three children under the root node:

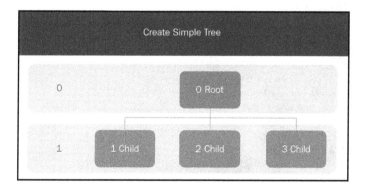

Figure 5

Consider the following code:

```
...
import pydot
import matplotlib.image as mpimg
import matplotlib.pyplot as plt

#create graph object
graph = pydot.Dot(graph_type='graph', dpi = 300)


#create and add root node
rootNode = pydot.Node("0 Root", style="filled", fillcolor = "#00ee11",
xlabel = "0")
graph.add_node(rootNode)
...
```

We have created a Python module called `TreePlotTest.py`, and have imported the `pydot` library and the required classes from `matplotlib`. Using the `Dot()` method of `pydot`, we can create a `graph` object that will hold the nodes and edges of the graph. We have also specified the `dpi` for the image as `300` in this case. We can use the `Node()` method of `pydot` to create a node. We are creating the `rootNode` by passing the label as `0 Root`, and using the `style` argument `filled` and the `fillcolor` argument `#00ee11`; the `xlabel` is `0`.

The `fillcolor` argument is specified in hexadecimal format. Browse to `https://www.w3schools.com/colors/colors_picker.asp` to select a color and see its hexadecimal code; later, you'll understand why the `xlabel` is used:

```
...
rootNode = pydot.Node("0 Root", style="filled", fillcolor = "#00ee11",
xlabel = "0")
graph.add_node(rootNode)

for i in range(3):
    #create node and add node
    childNode = pydot.Node("%d Child" % (i+1), style="filled", \
        fillcolor = "#ee0011", xlabel = "1")
    graph.add_node(childNode)
    #create edge between two nodes
    edge = pydot.Edge(rootNode, childNode)
    #add the edge to graph
    graph.add_edge(edge)
...
```

After we have created this `rootNode`, it will be added to the `graph` object, and we will create the `childNode` three times with appropriate names. The `style` argument will be `filled` with another color, and the `xlabel` will be 1. We will also add this node to the graph. Then, we will create an edge between the `rootNode` and the newly created `childNode`, and add this edge to the `graph` object. The snippet of code at the end of the following block is used to display the graph in full screen:

```
...
#show the diagram
graph.write_png('graph.png')
img=mpimg.imread('graph.png')
plt.imshow(img)
plt.axis('off')
mng = plt.get_current_fig_manager()
mng.window.state('zoomed')
plt.show()
...
```

Let's run the preceding code, and see what happens:

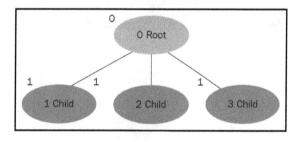

Figure 6

Upon successful execution of the code, we will see the four nodes: the root node, and then the three child nodes beneath it. We can see the xlabel values 0 and 1, which are extra annotations for the node.

Now, let's try modifying the name of the `childNode`. We will remove the numerical value from the child node's name, so that all three of the nodes have the same name:

```
...
for i in range(3):
    #create node and add node
    childNode = pydot.Node("%d Child", style="filled", \
        fillcolor = "#ee0011", xlabel = "1")
    graph.add_node(childNode)
...
```

Having made these changes to the names of the `childNode`, we will see the following:

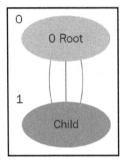

Figure 7

Since the three nodes have the same name, `pydot` treats them as the same node. Hence, we should try to use unique names in the nodes for the search tree. The following diagram shows an example of a search tree:

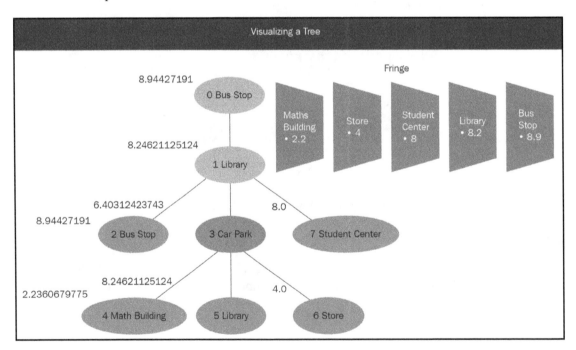

Figure 8

In the preceding diagram, we want to visualize a heuristic search. Each node has a heuristic value. In this example, **Bus Stop** appears twice, so we use index values to differentiate multiple instances. Each node also has a color code. Green nodes have already been explored; in this case, **Bus Stop** and **Library** will be explored. The red node has been selected for exploration; in this case, **Car Park** has been selected for exploration. The blue nodes are unexplored, forming a fringe, and they are arranged in a priority queue in descending order of heuristic values. A **fringe** is a priority queue of unexplored nodes, ordered by heuristic value.

In our case, the **Maths Building** comes first, because it has the lowest heuristic value (**2.2**), followed by **Store,** which has a heuristic value of **4**; **Student Center,** with a value of **8**; **Library,** with a value of **8.2**; and **Bus Stop,** with a value of **8.9**.

In DFS, we use the stack data structure, giving preference to the child nodes. In BFS, we use the queue data structure, giving preference to siblings. In a heuristic search, we will use the priority queue; this will give preference to the unexplored node that is closest to the goal, which is the first node in the priority queue:

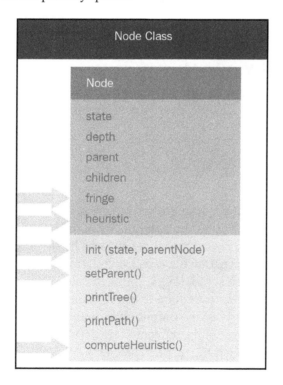

Figure 9

A few changes need to be made to the `Node` class in order to accommodate the heuristic search and visualization process. A new property called `fringe` is introduced, to indicate whether the node is a part of the fringe. A new property called `heuristic` is introduced, the constructor has changed, and an additional argument, `parentNode`, is introduced. The `addChild` method is changed to the `setParent` method, and we have a new method, called `computeHeuristic`. Now, let's take a look at the code for the `Node` class, as follows:

```
...
def __init__(self, state, parentNode):
    """
    Constructor
    """
    self.state = state
    self.depth = 0
    self.children = []
    #self.parent = None
    self.setParent(parentNode)
    self.fringe = True
    #self.heuristic
    self.computeHeuristic()
def setParent(self, parentNode):
    """
    This method adds a node under another node
    """
    if parentNode != None:
        parentNode.children.append(self)
        self.parent = parentNode
        self.depth = parentNode.depth + 1
    else:
        self.parent = None
...
```

Here, we have commented out the code for setting the parent as `None`. Instead, we have the `setParent` method, which takes the parent node as an argument and sets the property. We have a property called `fringe`, which is set as `True` by default, and there is a new property, `heuristic`, which is set by the `computeHeuristic` function . As mentioned previously, `addChild` has been set to `setParent`, which takes `parentNode` as an argument. We check whether the parent node is not `None`; if it is not `None`, then the node is added to the `children` property of the parent node, and the `parent` property of the current node is set as `parentNode`; the current node depth is equal to `parentNode.depth` + 1. If `parentNode` is `None`, then the `parent` property is set to `None`:

```
...
def computeHeuristic(self):
    """
```

```
        This function computes the heuristic value of node
        """
        #find the distance of this state to goal state
        #goal location
        goalLocation = location["AI Lab"]
        #current location
        currentLocation = location[self.state.place]
        #difference in x coordinates
        dx = goalLocation[0] - currentLocation[0]
        #difference in y coordinates
        dy = goalLocation[1] - currentLocation[1]
    . . .
```

There is also a new method called `computeHeuristic`. This function sets the `heuristic` property to a value. We will see how this function actually works, and what it computes, in the *Greedy BFS* and *A* Search* sections:

```
. . .
class TreePlot:
    """
    This class creates tree plot for search tree
    """
    def __init__(self):
        """
        Constructor
        """
        # create graph object
        self.graph = pydot.Dot(graph_type='graph', dpi = 500)
        #index of node
        self.index = 0
    def createGraph(self, node, currentNode):
        """
        This method adds nodes and edges to graph object
        Similar to printTree() of Node class
        """
        # assign hex color
        if node.state.place == currentNode.state.place:
            color = "#ee0011"
        elif node.fringe:
            color = "#0011ee"
        else:
            color = "#00ee11"
    . . .
```

In the Python `TreePlot.py` module, we created a class called `TreePlot`, which is used to create a tree visualization of the `Node` class. This class has two properties: the first one is a `graph` object, and the other one is the `index` of the node. It has a method called `createGraph`, which adds nodes and edges to the `graph` object. The flow of this method is similar to `printTree`, as it is recursively called on its child nodes. This method takes the current node being processed and `currentNode` as an argument. `currentNode` is the node that is shown in red in *Figure 8*, **Car Park**. The `createGraph` method checks whether the node that we are processing has the same state as that of the `currentNode`, and, if it does, it assigns color red to it. If it is a part of the fringe, the color blue is assigned. If the node has been explored, the color green is assigned:

```
. . .
#create node
        parentGraphNode = pydot.Node(str(self.index) + " " + \
            node.state.place, style="filled", \
            fillcolor = color, xlabel = node.heuristic)
        self.index += 1
#add node
        self.graph.add_node(parentGraphNode)
    . . .
```

After assigning the hexadecimal color of the node, we will create the node and call it `parentGraphNode`. The label of the node is a combination of the index value and the state of the node, and the `xlabel` is the heuristic value of the node. After we have created this node, the value of the index will be incremented, and the node will be added to the graph:

```
. . .
#call this method for child nodes
        for childNode in node.children:
            childGraphNode = self.createGraph(childNode, currentNode)
            #create edge
            edge = pydot.Edge(parentGraphNode, childGraphNode)
            #add edge
            self.graph.add_edge(edge)
        return parentGraphNode
    . . .
```

For each of the `childNode` objects, we call the `self.createGraph` method and pass `childNode` and `currentNode`. So, when we call this on `childNode`, it should return the corresponding `pydot` node. Then, we can create an edge between `parentGraphNode` and `childGraphNode`. After creating this edge, we can add it to our `graph` object:

```python
...
def generateDiagram(self, rootNode, currentNode):
    """
    This method generates diagram
    """
    #add nodes to edges to graph
    self.createGraph(rootNode, currentNode)
    #show the diagram
    self.graph.write_png('graph.png')
    img=mpimg.imread('graph.png')
    plt.imshow(img)
    plt.axis('off')
    mng = plt.get_current_fig_manager()
    mng.window.state('zoomed')
    plt.show()
...
```

This class has another method, called `generateDiagram`, and it takes `rootNode` and `currentNode` as arguments. First, it generates the `graph` object containing all of the nodes and edges by calling the `createGraph` method, with `rootNode` as the first argument and `currentNode` as the second argument. Then, we have the same snippet that we earlier used to show the diagram. So, if you want to visualize a search tree, you have to instantiate an object of `TreePlot` and call the `generateDiagram` method:

```python
...
from Node import Node
from State import State
from TreePlot import TreePlot

initialState = State()
root = Node(initialState)

childStates = initialState.successorFunction()
for childState in childStates:
    childNode = Node(State(childState))
    root.addChild(childNode)

treeplot = TreePlot()
treeplot.generateDiagram(root, root)
...
```

In the Python `TreePlotTest2.py` module, we imported the necessary classes—`Node`, `State`, and `TreePlot`, and we are creating a sample tree with the root node and child nodes of the first level. We also created a `TreePlot` object and called the `generateDiagram` method, with the arguments `root` and `root`:

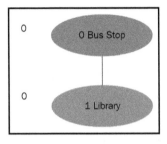

Figure 10

In the preceding diagram, we can see the root node and the first-level child node.

Now that you have learned how to visualize a tree, in the next section you will learn about greedy best-first search.

Greedy BFS

In the *Revisiting the navigation application* section, you learned that a heuristic value is a property of the node, and it is a guess, or estimate, of which node will lead to the goal state quicker than others. It is a strategy used to reduce the nodes explored and reach the goal state quicker. In **greedy BFS**, the heuristic function computes an estimated cost to reach the goal state. For our application, the heuristic function can compute the straight-line distance to the goal state, as follows:

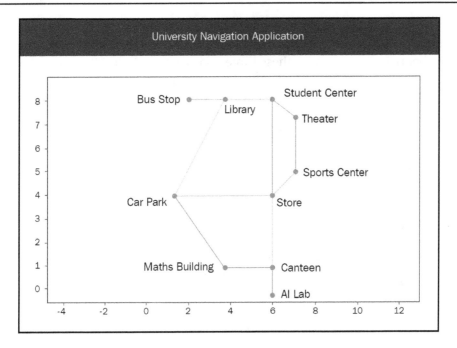

Figure 11

As you can see, in the preceding diagram the initial state is the **Bus Stop**. From the **Bus Stop** node, we have one channel, which is the **Library** node. Let's suppose that we're at the **Library** now; from the **Library** node, there are three child nodes: the **Car Park**, the **Bus Stop**, and the **Student Center**. In real life, we'd prefer to go to the **Car Park**, because it seems closer to the goal state, and the chances that we will reach the **AI Lab** faster are much higher:

```
...
#connections between places
connections = {}
connections["Bus Stop"] = {"Library"}
connections["Library"] = {"Bus Stop", "Car Park", "Student Center"}
connections["Car Park"] = {"Library", "Maths Building", "Store"}
connections["Maths Building"] = {"Car Park", "Canteen"}
connections["Student Center"] = {"Library", "Store" , "Theater"}
...
```

Let's use the location data of these four places (Library, Car Park, Bus Stop, and Student Center) to compute the heuristic functions for the three nodes. When you compute the heuristic functions for these three nodes, you will find that the value for Car Park is 6.4, Bus Stop is 8.9, and Student Center is 8.0. According to these heuristic values, we will select the first value in the fringe, which is the node with the lowest heuristic value (Car Park):

```
...
def computeHeuristic(self):
    """
    This function computes the heuristic value of node
    """
    #find the distance of this state to goal state
    #goal location
    goalLocation = location["AI Lab"]
    #current location
    currentLocation = location[self.state.place]
    #difference in x coordinates
    dx = goalLocation[0] - currentLocation[0]
    #difference in y coordinates
    dy = goalLocation[1] - currentLocation[1]
    #distance
    distance = math.sqrt(dx ** 2 + dy ** 2)
    print "heuristic for", self.state.place, "=", distance
    self.heuristic = distance
...
```

Let's take a look at the preceding computeHeuristic function. The Node class has a method called computeHeuristic. This function computes the heuristic value of the node by finding the distance from this state to the goal state. You can find the goal location by using the location dictionary of the navigation data and using the AI Lab as the key. You can find the current location by using the location dictionary, with the current place as the key. We find the difference in the x coordinates as follows: dx = goalLocation[0] - currentLocation[0]. We find the difference in the y coordinates as follows: dy = goalLocation[1] - currentLocation[1]. Finally, we compute the distance as the square root of dx square plus dy square, and we assign this distance to the heuristic property of the Node class:

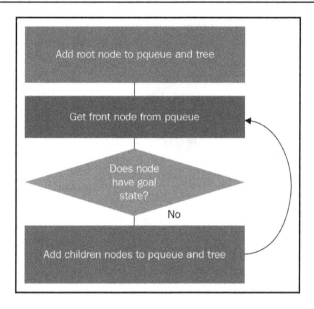

Figure 12

Now that you understand this heuristic function, let's look at the flow of the greedy BFS algorithm. The flow of this algorithm is similar to BFS. Instead of using a queue, we are going to use a priority queue, and we are going to compute the heuristic of the node and add the node, along with the heuristic value, to the priority queue:

1. We initially create the root node and add it to the tree, and then add this node, along with its heuristic value, to the priority queue.
2. We get the front node from the priority queue, and we check if it has goal state. If it does, we end our search here, and if it doesn't have the goal state, then we find its child nodes, add them to the tree, and then add them to the priority queue, along with a heuristic value.

3. We carry on with this process until we find the goal state or we've exhausted all of the nodes in our search stream.

Let's try to code the greedy BFS algorithm as follows:

```
...
def performGreedySearch():
    """
    This method performs greedy best first search
    """
    #create queue
    pqueue = Queue.PriorityQueue()
    #create root node
    initialState = State()
    #parent node of root is None
    root = Node(initialState, None)
    #show the search tree explored so far
    treeplot = TreePlot()
    treeplot.generateDiagram(root, root)
    #add to priority queue
    pqueue.put((root.heuristic, root))
        while not pqueue.empty():
        #get front node from the priority queue
        _, currentNode = pqueue.get()
        #remove from the fringe
        #currently selected for exploration
        currentNode.fringe = False
        print "-- current --", currentNode.state.place
...
```

In the Python `GreedySearch.py` module, we have created a `performGreedySearch()` method, which will perform the greedy BFS. In this method, we have created an empty priority queue for holding the nodes. With `initialState`, we are creating a root node, and, as mentioned earlier, the constructive node has changed; there is an additional argument in the parent node. For the root node, the parent node is `None`.

We are creating a `TreePlot` object and calling its `generateDiagram()` method to visualize the current search tree. In this case, the search tree will only contain the root node. We're adding the root node, along with its heuristic value, to the priority queue. We check whether the priority queue is not empty; if it is not empty, we get the front element and call it `currentNode`. As mentioned earlier, the format of the priority queue is a tuple containing the heuristic value and the node. Since we only want the node, we'll ignore the heuristic value. We will set the `fringe` property of `currentNode` to `False`, because it's currently selected for exploration:

```
...
#check if this is goal state
        if currentNode.state.checkGoalState():
            print "reached goal state"
```

```
            #print the path
            print "----------------------"
            print "Path"
            currentNode.printPath()
            #show the search tree explored so far
            treeplot = TreePlot()
            treeplot.generateDiagram(root, currentNode)
            break
#get the child nodes
        childStates = currentNode.state.successorFunction()
        for childState in childStates:
            #create node
            #and add to tree
            childNode = Node(State(childState), currentNode)
            #add to priority queue
            pqueue.put((childNode.heuristic, childNode))
        #show the search tree explored so far
        treeplot = TreePlot()
        treeplot.generateDiagram(root, currentNode)
    ...
```

We check whether the current node has the goal state; if it has the goal state, we print the path from the initial state to the goal state. We show the current search tree by calling the `treeplot.generateDiagram` method. If it doesn't have the goal state, we find the child states of the current node, and for each `childState`, we create the `childNode` by using the new constructor. In this new constructor, we pass the parent node as the `currentNode`, and we add the child node, along with its heuristic value, to the priority queue; we then display the current search tree.

So, we actually display the search tree at each step, whenever one level of the search tree is added. In this case, the search tree contains the root node. When one level of the search tree is added, we display the search tree; finally, when we reach the goal state, we prepare and then display the search tree that has been explored:

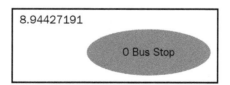

Figure 13

As you can see in the preceding output, we have a root node with the heuristic value 8.9 in our search tree. The Bus Stop node has been selected for exploration, and its child node library has been added to the search tree. The heuristic value of Library is 8.2, which is lower than the heuristic value of Bus Stop, which is 8.9. Since this is the only node in the fringe, it will be selected for exploration later:

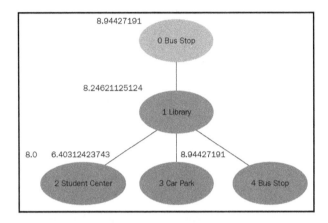

Figure 14

As shown in the preceding diagram, Library has been selected for exploration, and the child nodes of the Library node are added. We can see that for the three child nodes in the fringe, Bus Stop has a heuristic value of 8.9, Car Park has a heuristic value of 6.4, and Student Center has a heuristic value of 8.0. Out of the three nodes, Car Park has the lowest heuristic value, so this will be selected for exploration:

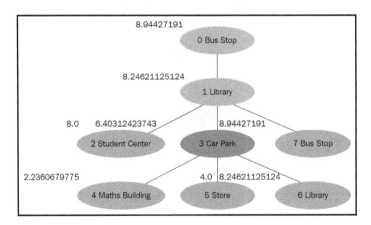

Figure 15

Now, Car Park has been selected for exploration, and its child nodes are added to the priority queue. Here, we have five nodes in the fringe. Bus Stop has a heuristic value of 8.9, the Maths Building has a heuristic value of 2.2, Library has a value of 8.2, Store has a value of 4, and Student Center has a value of 8.0. Of these five nodes, Maths Building has the lowest heuristic value (2.2), so it will be selected for exploration:

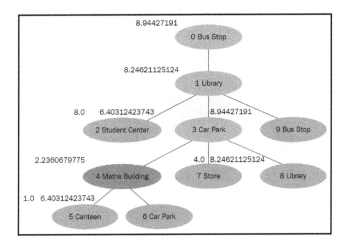

Figure 16

Now, Maths Building has been selected for exploration, and its child nodes are added to the search tree. Of the nodes in the fringe, Canteen has the lowest heuristic value (1.0), so it will be selected for exploration:

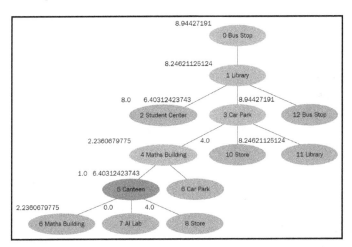

Figure 17

Now, the `Canteen` node has been selected for exploration, and its child nodes are added to the search tree and to the fringe. Out of all of the blue nodes, `AI Lab` has the lowest heuristic value (`0.0`), so it will be selected for exploration:

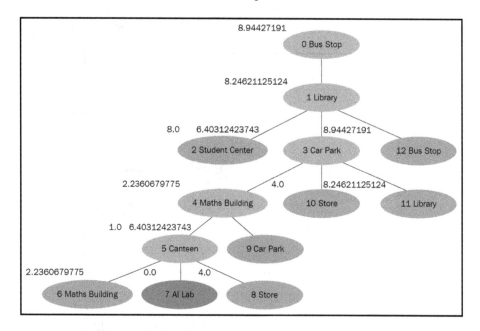

Figure 18

Finally, the `AI Lab` is selected for processing, and we find that we've reached the goal state, so we end our search here. The optimal path is shown by the green nodes and by the red node. The optimal path is `Bus Stop`, `Library`, `Car Park`, `Maths Building`, `Canteen`, and `AI Lab`.

As we go from the initial state to the goal state, we can observe that the heuristic values reduce. `Bus Stop` has the value `8.9`, `Library` has the value `8.2`, `Car Park` has the value `6.4`, `Maths Building` has the value `2.2`, `Canteen` has the value `1`, and `AI Lab` has the value `0`. This means that as we traverse the search tree, we are getting closer to the goal state. In the greedy BFS algorithm, the heuristic value reduces as we progress toward the goal state.

Now that you have learned the heuristic function for the greedy BFS algorithm, in the next section you will learn the problems with the greedy BFS algorithm, and you will see how A* Search solves those problems.

A* Search

In the preceding section, you learned that the path found by a greedy BFS is as follows:

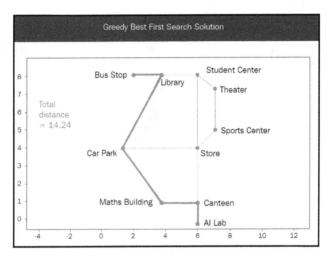

Figure 19

The total distance covered is **14.24**. However, the actual optimal solution is shown in the following diagram:

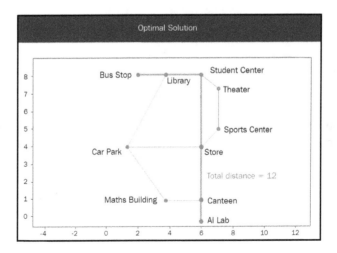

Figure 20

The total distance covered is **12**. This means that the greedy BFS algorithm is not optimal. The problem is that the heuristic function doesn't consider the costs already incurred. A* Search proposes a new heuristic function, which computes the sum of the cost incurred and the estimated cost to reach the goal state.

For our application, the heuristic function can compute the sum of the distance traveled from the root node to the current node, and the straight line distance to the goal state. Let's look at the example that we saw in the previous section and compute this new heuristic function for the three nodes **Car Park**, **Bus Stop**, and **Student Center**:

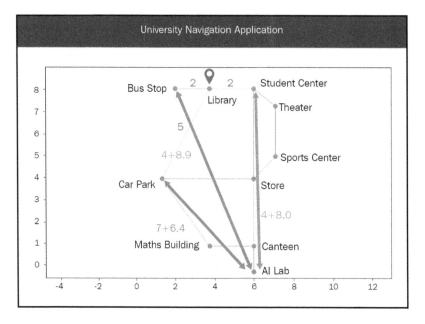

Figure 21

For the **Car Park**, the distance traveled is **2 + 5**, and the distance to the goal state is **6**, so the value of the new heuristic is **13.4**. For the **Bus Stop**, the distance traveled is **2 + 2**, which is **4**, and the distance to the goal state is **8.9**, so the value of the new heuristic function for the **Bus Stop** is **4 + 8.9**, which is **12.9**. For the **Student Center**, the distance traveled is **2 + 2**, which is **4**, and the distance to the goal state is **8**, so the value of the new heuristic function for the **Student Center** is **4 + 8**, which is **12**. Based on these new heuristic values, we will select **Student Center** for further exploration:

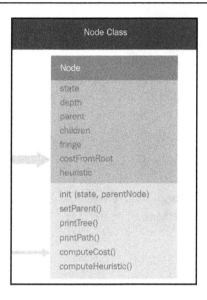

Figure 22

In addition to the changes to the `Node` class, which we saw in the *Visualizing a search tree* section, we will introduce a property called `costFromRoot` and a method called `computeCost`. The `costFromRoot` property is the distance incurred while traveling from the root node to the current node, and this value will be computed by the `computeCost` function:

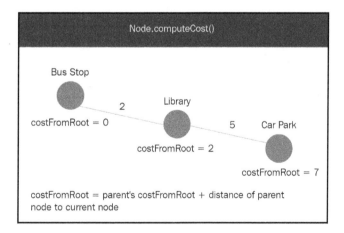

Figure 23

Let's look at how the `computeCost` method works. As indicated by the preceding diagram, we have three nodes: **Bus Stop**, **Library**, and **Car Park**. The distance between **Bus Stop** and **Library** is **2**, and the distance between **Library** and **Car Park** is **5**. Since **Bus Stop** is the initial state, the cost for that node is **0**. For **Library**, the cost from the root is **2**, and for **Car Park**, the `costFromRoot` is **2 + 5**, which is **7**. This is also the cost of its parent node plus the distance between the parent node and the current node. So, we can write the formula as follows:

costFromRoot = parent's costFromRoot + distance of parent node to current node

Let's look at the code for this method. Before we look at the `computeCost` method, let's look at the `computeDistance` method:

```
...
def computeDistance(self, location1, location2):
        """
        This method computes distance between two places
        """
        #difference in x coordinates
        dx = location1[0] - location2[0]
        #difference in y coordinates
        dy = location1[1] - location2[1]
        #distance
        distance = math.sqrt(dx ** 2 + dy ** 2)
        return distance
...
```

This method computes the distance between two locations, and it takes `location1` and `location2` as arguments. It finds the difference in the *x* coordinates as `dx` is equal to `location1[0] - location2[0]`, and it finds the difference in the *y* coordinates as `dy` is equal to `location1[1] - location2[1]`. It finds the distance as the square root of `dx` square plus `dy` square, and it returns this distance:

```
...
def computeCost(self):
        """
        This method computes distance of current node from root node
        """
        if self.parent != None:
            #find distance from current node to parent
            distance = self.computeDistance(location[self.state.place], \
                location[self.parent.state.place])
            #cost = parent cost + distance
            self.costFromRoot = self.parent.costFromRoot + distance
        else:
```

```
            self.costFromRoot = 0
    ...
```

The `computeCost` method computes the distance of the current node from the root node. So, we check whether the `parent` property is `None`. Then, we find the distance from the current location to the parent location, and we compute the `costFromRoot` as the parent's `costFromRoot` plus the distance that we've just computed; if the parent is `None`, then `costFromRoot` is 0, because this is the root node:

```
    ...
    def computeHeuristic(self):
        """
        This function computes the heuristic value of node
        """
        #find the distance of this state from goal state
        goalLocation = location["AI Lab"]
        currentLocation = location[self.state.place]
        distanceFromGoal = self.computeDistance(goalLocation,
        currentLocation)
        #add them up to form heuristic value
        heuristic = self.costFromRoot + distanceFromGoal
        print "heuristic for", self.state.place, "=",
        self.costFromRoot, distanceFromGoal, heuristic
        self.heuristic = heuristic
    ...
```

Now, let's look at the `computerHeuristic` method. Just like in a greedy BFS, we find the goal location as the location of the `AI Lab` and the current location, and we find the distance from the goal as the distance between the goal location and the current location. Then, we compute the heuristic as a sum of `costFromRoot` and `distanceFromGoal`, and we assign the `heuristic` property as this heuristic value:

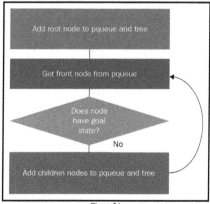

Figure 24

As shown in the preceding diagram, the flow of A* Search is actually the same as that of greedy BFS. So, let's look at the code for A* Search, as follows:

```
...
def performAStarSearch():
    """
    This method performs A* Search
    """
    #create queue
    pqueue = Queue.PriorityQueue()
    #create root node
    initialState = State()
    root = Node(initialState, None)
    #show the search tree explored so far
    treeplot = TreePlot()
    treeplot.generateDiagram(root, root)
    #add to priority queue
    pqueue.put((root.heuristic, root))
...
```

In the Python `AStar.py` module, we have created a method called `performAStarSearch`, which has the code for A* Search; this code is exactly the same as that of greedy BFS:

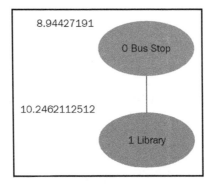

Figure 25

Initially, we have our root node with a heuristic value of `8.9`, and the `Bus Stop` node is selected for expansion; its `Library` child is added, and that has a heuristic value of `10.2`. Since this is the only node in the fringe, it will be selected for exploration:

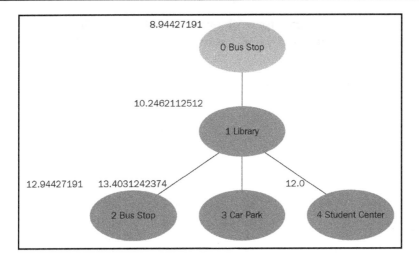

Figure 26

Now the `Library` node is selected for exploration, and its three child nodes are added. `Bus Stop` has a heuristic value of `12.9`, `Car Park` has a heuristic value of `13.4`, and `Student Center` has a heuristic value of `12`. Out of these three, `Student Center` has the lowest heuristic value, so it will be selected for exploration:

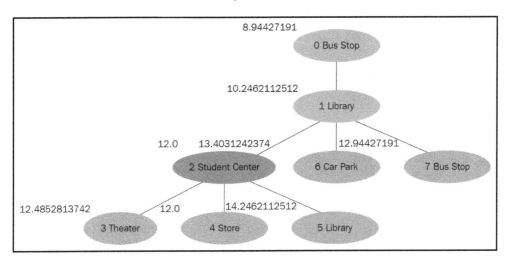

Figure 27

Now `Student Center` is selected for exploration, and its three child nodes are added to the fringe. Out of the five nodes in the fringe, `Store` has the lowest heuristic value, so it will be selected for exploration:

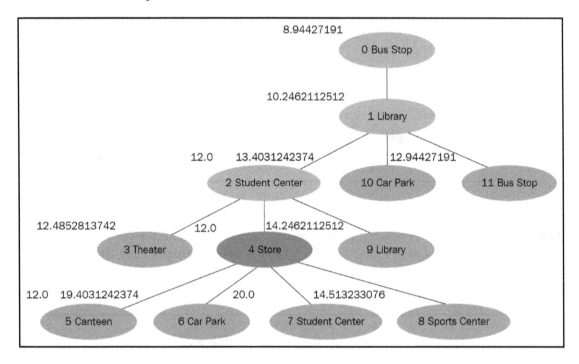

Figure 28

Now `Store` is selected for exploration, and its four child nodes are added. Out of the eight nodes in the fringe, `Canteen` has the lowest heuristic value, so it will be selected for exploration:

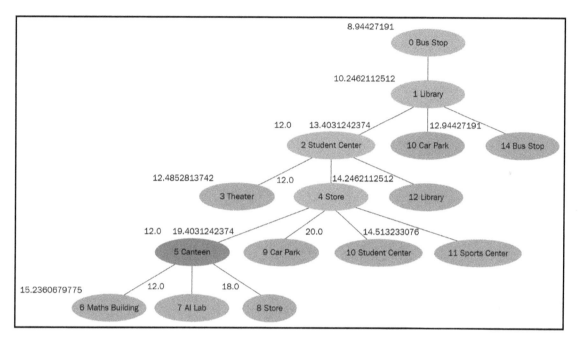

Figure 29

Now `Canteen` has been selected for exploration, and its child nodes are added to the search tree and to the fringe. Out of all of the nodes in the fringe, `AI Lab` has the lowest heuristic value, so this node will be selected for exploration:

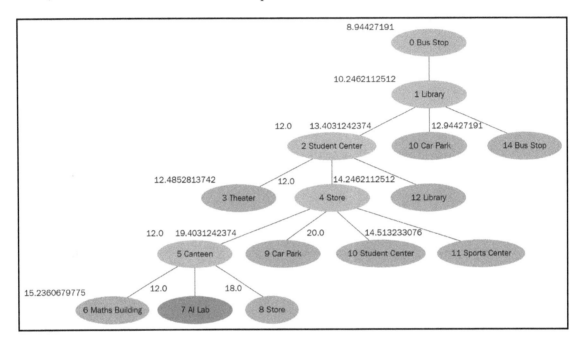

Figure 30

When `AI Lab` is select for exploration, we find that we've encountered the goal state, and we stop our search.

The optimal path is indicated by the green nodes and the red node. The optimal path is from `Bus Stop` to `Library` to `Student Center` to `Store` to `Canteen`, and finally to `AI Lab`. As we traverse from the root node to the goal node, we find that the heuristic function value either remains the same or increases. So, `Bus Stop` has the value 9, `Library` has the value 10.2, `Student Center` has the value 12.0, `Store` has the value 12.0, `Canteen` has the value 12.0, and finally `AI Lab` has the value 12.0. So, in this example, we learned that the heuristic function increases or remains the same as we progress from the initial state to the goal state, and we also observed that A* Search is optimal. We saw that greedy BFS is not optimal, and we can now understand why. We saw a new heuristic function, which makes A* optimal. In the next section, we will look at what a good heuristic function entails.

What is a good heuristic function?

To answer the question, *why is a good heuristic function required?* We will compare the DFS and BFS methods to the heuristic search approach. In DFS and BFS, the costs of all of the edges are equal to **1**, and DFS explores all of the child nodes, whereas BFS explores all of the sibling nodes. In a heuristic search, the costs of the edges are different, and the heuristic search selects the nodes to explore based on heuristic functions.

By using a heuristic function, we can reduce the memory that is used, and we can reach the solution in less time. The next question to be answered is, *why is a good heuristic function required?* The answer is in order to find the **optimal solution**. In our A* Search example, we illustrated that by using a better heuristic function, we can find the optimal solution; it is clear that A* explores the least number of nodes. Now, let's look at the properties of a good heuristic function.

Properties of a good heuristic function

The properties of a good heuristic functions are detailed in the following sections.

Admissible

A good heuristic function should be admissible, which means that the heuristic function should have a value that is less than (or equal to) the true cost to reach the goal:

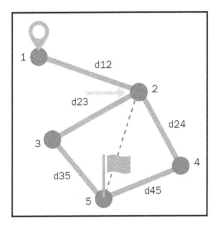

Figure 31

Let's suppose that node **1** is the root node and node **5** has the goal state, and we are currently computing the heuristic function for node **2**; the following applies:

- **d12** is the cost of the path from **1** to **2**
- **d24** is the cost of the path from node **2** to **4**
- **d45** is the cost from node **4** to **5**
- **d23** is the cost from node **2** to **3**
- **d35** is the cost from node **3** to **5**

Then, in order for our function to be admissible, the following must be true:

- The heuristic function for node **2** should have a value less than or equal to **d24 + d45**
- The heuristic function for node **2** should have a value less than or equal to **d23 + d35**

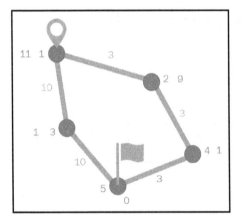

Figure 32

In the preceding example, node **1** is the root node and node **5** has the goal state. The red values are the estimated cost to the goal state, and the green values are the true cost of the edge:

1. Let's suppose that we have explored node **1**, and have added nodes **2** and **3** to the fringe. So, we will compute the heuristic values for nodes **2** and **3**.
2. The heuristic value for node **2** is **3 + 9**, which is **12**, and the heuristic value for node **3** is **10 + 1**, which is **11**; based on these values, we select node **3** for further exploration.

3. We add the child of node **3**, which is node **5**, to the fringe. The fringe contains nodes **2** and **5**. We had previously computed the heuristic function for node **2** as **12**, and the heuristic function for node **5** as **10 + 10 + 0**, which is **20**. So, based on these values, we will select node **2** for exploration.

4. We add the child of node **2**, which is node **4**, to the fringe. Now, the fringe contains **4** and **5**. We had previously computed the heuristic function for node **5** as **20**, and we will compute the heuristic function for node **4** as **3 + 3 + 1**, which is **7**. Based on these values, we will select node **4** for further exploration.

5. We add the child of node **4**, which is node **5**, to the fringe. The fringe contains node **5** through path [1-3-5], and node **5** through path [1-2-4-5]. We had previously computed the heuristic function for node **5** through path [1-3-5] as **20**. So, we compute the heuristic function of node **5** through path [1-2-4-5] as **3 + 3 + 3 + 0**, which is **9**. Based on these values, we select node **5** with path [1-2-4-5]; when we process this node, we see that we've reached the goal state and end our search here.

In this example, you saw that during the search process, we side-tracked to node **3**. Later, we found the optimal solution to be [1-2-4-5]. So, an admissible heuristic guaranteed finding the optimal solution.

Consistent

The second property a good heuristic function should have is that it should be consistent, which means that it should be non-decreasing:

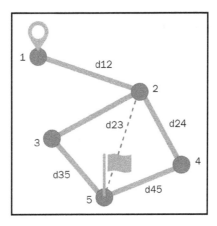

Figure 33

For example, the heuristic function for node **3** should be greater than (or equal to) the heuristic function for node **2**, and the value of the heuristic function for node **4** should be greater than (or equal to) the value of the heuristic function for node **2**. Let's look at why this is so, through the following diagram:

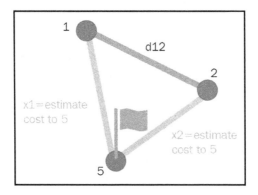

Figure 34

Let's suppose that nodes **1** and **2** are intermediate nodes, and node **5** has the goal state. First, **x1** is the estimated cost of node **1** to node **5**, and **x2** is the estimated cost of reaching the goal state from node **2**; **d12** is the cost of going from node **1** to node **2**.

Let's suppose that node **2** is closer to the goal state than node **1**; this means that the following statement applies:

```
x2 < x1
```

Suppose that the following statement is true:

```
x2 =100
x1= 101
d12 >= 1
```

The preceding code means that $x1 <= d12 + x2$.

Suppose that TC1 is the true cost of reaching node **1** from the root node; then, the heuristic function for node 1 will be as follows:

```
h(1) =TC1 + x1
```

The heuristic function for node **2** will be as follows:

```
h(2) = TC1 + d12 + x2
```

This is because $d12 + x2 >= x1$; the heuristic value of **2** is greater than or equal to the value of the heuristic function for node **1** (that is, $h(2) >= h(1)$).

Summary

You should now understand what a heuristic function is, and also the priority queue data structure. In this chapter, you learned how to visualize search trees. You learned the heuristic function for a greedy best-first search and the steps involved in this algorithm. We also covered problems related to the greedy best-first algorithm, and how an A* Search solves them. Finally, you learned the properties required for a good heuristic function.

 Please refer to the link `https://www.packtpub.com/sites/default/files/downloads/HandsOnArtificialIntelligenceforSearch_ColorImages.pdf` for the colored images of this chapter.

Other Books You May Enjoy

If you enjoyed this book, you may be interested in these other books by Packt:

Artificial Intelligence for Big Data
Anand Deshpande, Manish Kumar

ISBN: 978-1-78847-217-3

- Manage Artificial Intelligence techniques for big data with Java
- Build smart systems to analyze data for enhanced customer experience
- Learn to use Artificial Intelligence frameworks for big data
- Understand complex problems with algorithms and Neuro-Fuzzy systems
- Design stratagems to leverage data using Machine Learning process
- Apply Deep Learning techniques to prepare data for modeling
- Construct models that learn from data using open source tools
- Analyze big data problems using scalable Machine Learning algorithms

Artificial Intelligence By Example

Denis Rothman

ISBN: 978-1-78899-054-7

- Use adaptive thinking to solve real-life AI case studies
- Rise beyond being a modern-day factory code worker
- Acquire advanced AI, machine learning, and deep learning designing skills
- Learn about cognitive NLP chatbots, quantum computing, and IoT and blockchain technology
- Understand future AI solutions and adapt quickly to them
- Develop out-of-the-box thinking to face any challenge the market presents

Leave a review - let other readers know what you think

Please share your thoughts on this book with others by leaving a review on the site that you bought it from. If you purchased the book from Amazon, please leave us an honest review on this book's Amazon page. This is vital so that other potential readers can see and use your unbiased opinion to make purchasing decisions, we can understand what our customers think about our products, and our authors can see your feedback on the title that they have worked with Packt to create. It will only take a few minutes of your time, but is valuable to other potential customers, our authors, and Packt. Thank you!

Index

A

A* Search 93, 94, 95, 96, 97, 98, 99, 100, 101, 102

B

basic search concepts
  goal function 16
  initial state 16
  node 17
  state 16
  successor function 16
BFS, versus DFS
  data structures 64
  memory 64
  optimal solution 65
  order of traversal 63
breadth-first search (BFS) algorithm 45, 57, 59, 60, 61, 62

C

cycle 51

D

dequeue 56
DFS algorithm
  about 29, 30, 31, 32, 34
  recursive DFS 35, 36
dictionary 52

E

edges 51
enqueue 56

F

Fibonacci sequence
  example 37
file searching applications 14, 15
first in first out (FIFO) 56

G

goal function 16
graph 51, 52, 53
Graphviz
  about 75
  download link 5
  setting up 8, 9, 10, 11
greedy BFS 84, 85, 86, 87, 88, 89, 90, 91, 92

H

heuristic 69, 72
heuristic function
  about 103
  admissible 103, 104, 105
  consistent 105, 106
  properties 103

I

initial state 16

L

last-in first-out (LIFO) 27
libraries
  installing 5
  setting up 5
LinkedIn connection feature 46, 47, 48, 49, 50

M

Matplotlib 6

N

nodes
  about 17, 51
  trees, building 22, 23, 24, 25, 26, 27

P

pip
  about 6
  installing 12, 13
priority queue
  about 72, 73
  dequeue operation 73
  get front element operation 73
  insert operation 73
Pydot 6
Python 2.7.6
  download link 6
Python libraries
  download link 5
Python
  setting up 6, 7, 8

Q

queue 55, 56

R

recursive DFS
  implementing 39, 40, 41, 42, 43
  steps 37

S

search problem
  formulating 17, 18, 19, 21
search tree
  visualizing 75, 76, 77, 78, 79, 80, 81, 82, 83
stack
  about 27, 28
  pop operation 27
  push operation 27
state 16
successor function 16

T

trees
  about 51
  building, with nodes 22, 23, 24, 25, 26, 27

U

university navigation application
  about 70, 72
  developing 66, 67, 68

www.ingramcontent.com/pod-product-compliance
Lightning Source LLC
Chambersburg PA
CBHW080538060326
40690CB00022B/5165